Cambridge Elements

Elements of Sustainability: Science, Policy, Practice
Series Editor-in-Chief
Arun Agrawal
University of Notre Dame

A BIT TOO SIMPLE

Narratives of Development, Sustainability and Climate Change

Mette Fog Olwig
Roskilde University

Shaftesbury Road, Cambridge CB2 8EA, United Kingdom

One Liberty Plaza, 20th Floor, New York, NY 10006, USA

477 Williamstown Road, Port Melbourne, VIC 3207, Australia

314–321, 3rd Floor, Plot 3, Splendor Forum, Jasola District Centre, New Delhi – 110025, India

103 Penang Road, #05–06/07, Visioncrest Commercial, Singapore 238467

Cambridge University Press is part of Cambridge University Press & Assessment, a department of the University of Cambridge.

We share the University's mission to contribute to society through the pursuit of education, learning and research at the highest international levels of excellence.

www.cambridge.org
Information on this title: www.cambridge.org/9781009714013

DOI: 10.1017/9781009344944

© Mette Fog Olwig 2025

This publication is in copyright. Subject to statutory exception and to the provisions of relevant collective licensing agreements, with the exception of the Creative Commons version the link for which is provided below, no reproduction of any part may take place without the written permission of Cambridge University Press & Assessment.

An online version of this work is published at doi.org/10.1017/9781009344944 under a Creative Commons Open Access license CC-BY-NC 4.0 which permits re-use, distribution and reproduction in any medium for non-commercial purposes providing appropriate credit to the original work is given and any changes made are indicated. To view a copy of this license visit https://creativecommons.org/licenses/by-nc/4.0

When citing this work, please include a reference to the DOI 10.1017/9781009344944

First published 2025

A catalogue record for this publication is available from the British Library

ISBN 978-1-009-71401-3 Hardback
ISBN 978-1-009-34491-3 Paperback
ISSN 2635-0211 (online)
ISSN 2635-0203 (print)

Cambridge University Press & Assessment has no responsibility for the persistence or accuracy of URLs for external or third-party internet websites referred to in this publication and does not guarantee that any content on such websites is, or will remain, accurate or appropriate.

For EU product safety concerns, contact us at Calle de José Abascal, 56, 1°, 28003 Madrid, Spain, or email eugpsr@cambridge.org

A Bit Too Simple

Narratives of Development, Sustainability and Climate Change

Elements of Sustainability: Science, Policy, Practice

DOI: 10.1017/9781009344944
First published online: September 2025

Mette Fog Olwig
Roskilde University

Author for correspondence: Mette Fog Olwig, mettefo@ruc.dk

Abstract: Narratives like those portraying development workers as heroes and local populations as victims needing to be saved from their own unsustainable practices have led to problematic policies and interventions. Based on fieldwork across four continents, this Element critically analyzes such metanarratives. First, it demonstrates the ways their simplifying, universalistic narrative plots fail to capture more complex lived realities. Second, it argues that such metanarratives on development are converging with influential metanarratives on climate change and sustainability, thereby strengthening hierarchical geopolitical mindsets. Third, it uncovers how the emergence of for-profit sustainability superhero metanarratives reinforces universalistic development logics by combining them with global business management logics. The Element concludes that a multiplicity of locally grounded stories and related forms of agency must be mobilized and recognized so that policy and practice are premised upon lived realities, not abstract and unrealistic global imaginaries. This title is also available as open access on Cambridge Core.

Keywords: climate change, environmental narratives, sustainable development, climate disasters, development discourse

© Mette Fog Olwig 2025

ISBNs: 9781009714013 (HB), 9781009344913 (PB), 9781009344944 (OC)
ISSNs: 2635-0211 (online), 2635-0203 (print)

Contents

1 Introduction: A Bit Too Simple?   1

2 Crisis, A Call to Action: The Making of Floods into Disasters   18

3 Villains, Victims and Heroes: The Cast of Characters and Their Roles in Environmental Decline   26

4 Solutions: How Trees Became the Answer to Climate Change   36

5 For-Profit Characters and Storylines: Sustainability Superheroes and Profitable Redemption   48

6 Conclusion: Mobilizing Grounded Stories   61

References   68

1 Introduction: A Bit Too Simple?

"Trees are good," "floods are bad" and "locals are helpless." Such unnuanced ideas are often fostered by influential metanarratives that contradict the complexity of scientific findings and are inconsistent with the multiplicity of grounded experiences. Yet, through time they have underpinned many development, sustainability and climate change interventions with problematic consequences.

A narrative is a story about events in which the storyline has a beginning, middle and end that connects the events as a plot, thereby making it possible to reduce what may in fact be a complex and entangled bundle of events into a simplified linear storyline. Shared narratives that provide socially significant accounts of events are an integral part of human society and can "have the objective of getting their hearers to believe or do something" (Roe 1991, p. 288). This would often be the moral of the story. While many people are unaware of the existence and effect of such narratives, the unconscious and implicit use of narratives is at times key to facilitating action according to specific values (Adger et al. 2001; Lejano & Nero 2020; Roe 1991). Locally devised narratives are common and innate to human societies and can play an important role in creating communal cohesion and belonging, but these narratives do not tend to drive international action. Instead, problematic overarching metanarratives have emerged that build on a long legacy of geopolitical storytelling that has spoken to and been propelled across the world by elites such as colonial and postcolonial officers, missionaries, practitioners and administrators. In this Element, I will analyze such geopolitical metanarratives in the context of development, sustainability and climate change.

A geopolitical storyline that continues to show up in different metanarratives of development is that of the "White Man's Burden." This was the title of an (in)famous 1899 poem by the English author Rudyard Kipling. *The White Man's Burden* refers to the construed moral obligation of the heroic "White Man" to "civilize" the "Non-White Other," thereby providing the rationale for imperialism and colonialism that exacerbated inequalities worldwide. Through time, many development narratives have followed a similarly moralistic mission where heroic development practitioners are portrayed as burdened with the responsibility to save the "other" by teaching them better ways.

Villains, victims and heroes are popular figures in storytelling, as is apparent from the ubiquity of the plot of the "hero's journey." In this storyline, the hero is called to action (e.g., because of a crisis), sometimes referred to as "the call to adventure," and embarks on a journey to "a distant land" (Campbell 1949, p. 58). Here the protagonist overcomes various challenges, which could include defeating a villain, and once victorious is able to travel back home as a hero

(Ascough 2018, p. 535). The hero's journey is a common feature in colonial and postcolonial development narratives (Ascough 2018). Local people have, for example, been implicitly cast as the villains when they engage in practices that are often misleadingly linked to environmental destruction, such as (implicitly immoral) swidden agriculture, agroforestry and forest grazing (Benjaminsen 2021; Leach & Mearns 1996). In such narratives, the local population usually has a double role, as they are often also made to play the role of helpless victims who are suffering from the environmental destruction and need to be saved by the hero. Here, I will refer to these particular hero narratives as "development hero metanarratives."

The storyline of development hero metanarratives is simple and typically begins with an imagined idealized normal condition, challenged by a disruptive environmental crisis caused by local resource mismanagement that requires action in order to be solved. The crisis in this simple storyline thus provides a "call to action" for the "heroic" development practitioner to "civilize" and thereby "save" the "natives" by teaching them how to change their customary practices (Ferguson 1994; Mutua 2001). At the same time, however, such narratives effectively devalue local understandings of environmental problems and knowledge of possible solutions (Leach & Mearns 1996). The metanarratives that become predominant worldwide are not necessarily the ones that generate the most effective or equitable solutions. In relation to the development sector, they tend to be those that challenge the status quo the least by obscuring underlying structural inequalities.

Over the years, while conducting research on climate change, disasters and sustainability, I have been struck by the prevalence of some remarkably similar narratives that I kept encountering across quite different national and societal contexts. They were similar because they were linked to the same overarching development hero metanarratives just described. In 2010, while doing fieldwork on climate change and flooding disasters in Bolgatanga in northern Ghana, I witnessed a climate change school event (see Figure 1) arranged by international volunteers that illustrates this well. The disruptive crisis in the storyline of the event is climate change, which is threatening the local people (the "victims"), and the solution is changing local practices. The school children held placards that read "climate change" followed by "stop bush burning," "pick up litter and recycle," "plant more trees," "every tree matters" or "look after your community." This means, in effect, that the (unwitting) "villains" are those community members who continue bush burning and littering, and who fail to plant trees ("uncivilized" local behavior). The "heroes" are the international volunteers who were called to action and arranged the event for the school children and sensitized them to the importance of changing local behavior. The metanarrative that is enacted and sometimes even internalized by the enactors, in this case the local people and the international volunteers, has the underlying implication that local actions are to blame for environmental problems and that external heroes are needed if local people are to be saved from themselves.

When I asked a local Ghanaian friend watching the event what it was all about, he replied: "It is about picking up litter. Our climate is changing, and if we don't pick up rubber [plastic], the climate will change" (diary, Bolgatanga, Ghana, March 2010). Avoiding littering is positive, but by suggesting that local people can induce climate change through littering, the event subtly conflated climate change with separate local challenges. Meanwhile, attention was deflected from important wider societal and physical trends across large distances – or teleconnections – leading to climate vulnerability and climate variability, such as the effects of global commodity markets and the El Niño (Adger et al. 2009; Moser & Hart 2015). Additionally, underlying local issues were sidetracked. When walking around Bolgatanga, it was evident that one of the main types of litter in the streets was plastic from 500 ml water sachets. In Figure 1, these sachets can be seen sticking out from the big black trash bags. Compared to water bottles, water sachets provided a cheaper source of water and were therefore popular in an area where many did not have access to running water let alone filtered and sanitized drinking water. Yet, water sachets produced a type of waste that did not decompose.

Figure 1 Climate change event in Bolgatanga, Ghana, March 2010.
Photo by author.

Furthermore, they were not always as hygienic as their nickname "pure water" promised. Ensuring easier access to water and sanitation would therefore be an important component of addressing the water sachet bag/littering problem. Similarly, encouraging the local population to plant trees can be a good idea, but, as I will show in Section 4, if this leads to undifferentiated and monocrop tree planting, it can be a bad idea. Thus, while development hero metanarratives incline to blame local actions for environmental destruction, such storylines often turn out to be much too simple.

Drawing on ethnographic research in Ghana, Vietnam, Tanzania, the USA and Denmark, *A Bit Too Simple* highlights and analyzes the different ways in which development sector professionals, businesspersons, government employees and local people in widely diverse parts of the world are affected by, respond to and challenge, but also perpetuate, the same circulating hegemonizing development hero metanarratives.[1] The Element focuses in particular on development hero metanarratives concerning environmental challenges. Development and environmental agendas have been officially interlinked through the notion of sustainable development since the 1987 United Nations (UN) Brundtland Report (Brundtland 1987). With the 2015 ratification of the UN development framework known as the Sustainable Development Goals (SDGs), global social, economic and environmental challenges all fell under the rubric of "sustainable development." As the UN explained, "ending poverty and other deprivations must go hand-in-hand with strategies that improve health and education, reduce inequality, and spur economic growth – all while tackling climate change and working to preserve our oceans and forests."[2] Development, sustainability and climate change were thereby subsumed under the same universalistic framework. To include all these challenges in one universally applicable framework, the SDGs ended up reducing complex phenomena to 17 goals and 169 targets that could be universally tracked, measured and even monetized through business-oriented management logics. It is within this context of increasingly universalizing and managerial simplification of development logics that the analysis is situated.

The Element will make three key arguments. *First*, it reveals how simplifying, universalistic development hero metanarratives can define agendas for action toward the environment that fail to capture lived realities, and which can lead to problematic policy and practice. In this way, the Element is a critical analysis of

---

[1] This Element brings together research that I have conducted over a 15-year period and incorporates material (including interview quotes) previously published in Olwig (2021a, 2021b) and Olwig & Rasmussen (2016).

[2] https://sdgs.un.org/goals (accessed July 2, 2025).

metanarratives in light of locally grounded stories and experiences. *Second*, it argues that long-standing development hero metanarratives are converging with other influential metanarratives on climate change and sustainability, thereby strengthening hierarchical geopolitical mindsets that can further inequality and inefficiency in efforts to promote sustainability. *Third*, it shows how for-profit hero metanarratives on sustainable development are emerging that reinforce universalistic development logics through integrating them with global business management logics.

The Element concludes that there is a need for the recognition and active mobilization of a greater variety of stories that are grounded in a diversity of specific experiences in order to counter simplifying, universalistic metanarrative storylines. Such locally grounded stories are essential because they can inform solutions that recognize a variety of underlying structural issues and address complex socio-environmental problems.

Stories, Narratives and Metanarratives

The science on development, sustainability and climate change challenges can seem abstract, complex and obscure. This is in part because these challenges often cross borders or entail time horizons that can be difficult to comprehend. This may lead to a sense of frustration and even apathy, immobilization and despair. Translating the findings of scientific research on such challenges into policy and practice therefore necessarily involves making the science more accessible. Here, coherent and compelling narratives can play a key role. An important dimension of a narrative is that it "takes the otherwise inchoate things, events, and places in a novel (or a life) and makes everything fit together" (Lejano & Nero 2020, p. 8). Or, as the anthropologist Edward Bruner succinctly puts it: "Stories make meaning" (Bruner 1986, p. 140). Importantly, not any "set of random, haphazard utterances" constitute a narrative, rather they must be part of a coherent storyline so that they appear to "describe a logical set of ideas or sequence of events" (Lejano & Nero 2020, p. 8).

Some narratives become so dominant that they turn into hegemonizing metanarratives, such as the development hero metanarratives introduced earlier. Narratives have been important in the development sector as a way to allay uncertainties and simplify challenges, thereby enabling practitioners, local administrators, civil servants and policymakers to formulate implementable policy and practice in the face of complicated issues (Roe 1991, p. 288). In the following I distinguish between, on the one hand, what I call *locally grounded stories* that concern particular sets of events occurring in specific places and, on the other, what I call *metanarratives*. What makes a narrative "meta" is its overarching universalistic character, which, in this context, it has taken on in prominent discourses within sectors that operate around the world such as the international development sector (see also Lejano & Nero 2020).

Overarching development metanarratives are not grounded in specific local stories, even if they at times may make use of them. Rather, they are rooted in universalistic rationalities. As a result, they can travel between regions and countries and often become dominant worldwide through the influence of the international development sector (Mosse 2011; Olwig 2013; Roe 1991). The metanarratives that become dominant are not necessarily the most logical or the ones that are supported by evidence on the ground (Lejano & Nero 2020; Roe 1991). Indeed, the validity of a narrative has often proven irrelevant to whether it gains traction (Lejano & Nero 2020; Roe 1991). The logic of a narrative is combined with other elements, such as the emotional, aesthetic and moral, that can be more powerful than scientific logic (Lejano & Nero 2020). Narratives, as such, are not especially amenable to scientific quantitative explanations. The analysis of narratives belongs rather to the field of the humanities and its concern with interpretive understanding. This does not mean that an analysis of narratives is anti-scientific. As used here, the narrative analysis draws considerably on scientific evidence to show how what might be perceived as being science may have been unwittingly influenced by metanarratives coming from outside the sciences.

Grounded stories are relayed by various actors who may tell differing, complementary stories to, for example, explain and interpret why some people are more vulnerable to environmental disasters than others. Taking the example of flooding disasters in northern Ghana, local stories might thus describe how those without any close relatives nearby are more vulnerable to flooding disasters than those with family networks in the area. There might also be stories of select people receiving cement from nongovernmental organizations (NGOs) and therefore being able to improve their houses so they were less likely to collapse during floods (Olwig 2013). The universalistic metanarratives, by contrast, are not based on the local people's various experiences in specific local contexts. They refer to, and are shaped by, a generalized and globalized world view based on "shared myths and blueprints of the world" (Adger et al. 2001, p. 683). In relation to flooding disasters, or disasters in general, an example could be the globalized world view that women, children and people with disabilities are the most vulnerable. As a result, these categories are often targeted by NGOs. This view is not necessarily shared in all local communities, however. As a local politician (an assemblyman) explained to me during an interview:

> This word [vulnerability] people don't understand. You can get someone who has good eyes and he can't see. But you, the white people, you look at the

> person's structure, "oh, he is well-to-do." No! Here the vulnerable, you can see somebody who is very fit, but he is vulnerable ... [I]f you are blind and you have children who can take care of you, you are better off than someone who has eyes and who hasn't got someone to care for him. (Olwig 2013, pp. 440–441)

When development policies and projects draw on singular universalistic metanarratives and ignore locally grounded multiplicities of stories, this can lead to disconnected policies and practices that are unsuitable in specific local contexts (Adger et al. 2001; Marino & Ribot 2012). This does not mean that universalistic rationalities are always inappropriate (Olwig 2013). For example, when stakeholders are negotiating policy agreements at the Conference of the Parties (COP) to the UN Framework Convention on Climate Change (UNFCCC), universalistic rationalities can be useful, and it can be meaningful and necessary to discuss an estimated "average global temperature" as an indicator of the magnitude of the problem. Yet, this universalism, and the estimated average global temperature, is in some ways irrelevant in a particular place, where climate change adaptation depends on knowledge about the specific increase – or decrease – in temperature, and how this change will impact this place in terms of, for example, its distinct land use or infrastructure.

Narratives as Structures of Power

The telling of stories implicitly involves an element of entertainment, and in some stories, such as a fable, there is a moral of the story, which usually becomes explicit at the end. Such stories often utilize the emotional value of the familiar, and frequently build on mythological stories with ancient origins. These rhetorical devices make narratives persuasive at another level of comprehension, and narratives can thereby influence how different actors understand and choose to react to complicated challenges. In this way, while "classificatory schemes provide a science of the concrete, narrative schemes may provide a science of the imagination" (Bruner 1986, p. 141). A well-told story is thus a powerful story. A well-told overarching story – or metanarrative – is even more powerful.

Stories can be key to sustaining traditions and upholding communities and organizations (Lejano & Nero 2020, p. 2), but they can also uphold unequal power relations. Indeed, many development metanarratives that have emerged and been promoted have been in the interest of powerful actors. Since colonialism, problematic metanarratives on the need to rectify perceived local resource mismanagement have been instrumentalized to rationalize external intervention in relation to the use and control of natural resources, while downplaying political, structural and power dynamics (Leach & Mearns 1996, p. 20). The anthropologist James Ferguson argues that the development sector tends to frame challenges as requiring the apolitical, technical interventions that they claim they can provide (Ferguson 1994). This is what anthropologist Tania M. Li refers to as "rendering technical," whereby the development sector can avoid dealing with root causes (Li 2007). Similarly, in relation to climate change, the "adaptation concept slips insistently to technological measures" in part because this makes climate change appear more governable (Nightingale et al. 2020, p. 344). These external interventions are further often legitimized through an emphasis on emotional and moral motivations. Moreover, the external practitioners are regularly presented as apolitical, capable and responsible experts, while local people are positioned as incapable and lacking in knowledge (Mosurska et al. 2023, p. 188; see also Mikulewicz 2020). These metanarratives thereby posture as apolitical stories that reflect an objective reality. But in practice, their employment is in and of itself a very political act that can serve to uphold historical power relations between countries (Chouliaraki & Vestergaard 2022, p. 3; Kapoor 2008).

Development hero metanarratives tend to engender geographically determined reductive categories (cf. Said 1978) that can lead to a dichotomous North-South hierarchy where the South is presented as the subject and the North as the "active and benevolent provider of knowledge and material assistance" (Mawdsley 2017, p. 108). This is an outgrowth of a colonial division of the world that placed certain countries at the center of modernity and progress and others in "subordinate positions" (Mutua 2001, p. 204; see also Bhambra 2009; Sen 2020b). While this division was the rationale for imperial projects, the dichotomy prevails in many present-day development narratives and works to maintain the hierarchy between the North and the South. Equally, it discourages actors in the Global North[3] from critically examining the implications of their own lifestyle that depends on upholding the unequal geopolitical status quo originally established through colonialism and imperialism. As Bruner explains, narratives can become "structures of power," with problematic policy and political consequences (1986, p. 144).

Narratives as Disciplinary Power

Narratives do not just provide a simplifying framework for interpreting events, behavior and processes. They are also constitutive in the sense that they can

---

[3] I use the terms Global North and Global South, even though the terms are not without their problems. Being part of the Global North or the Global South does not necessarily indicate a country's or place's location on a map, but rather a country's positionality in the "global" order – in terms of geopolitical power relations including former colonial and current donor–aid relations.

construct events, behavior and processes. Development narratives, for example, have been described as "disciplining" in the Foucauldian sense of the word (Foucault 1978). The disciplinary power of these narratives can construct externally fundable subjects. For example, when the storyline emphasizes the need for climate adaptation, the local population in the story becomes externally fundable climate subjects (Lindegaard 2020; Mikulewicz 2020; Mills-Novoa et al. 2020, 2023). Such disciplining development metanarratives are furthermore able to hegemonize imaginaries because they are communicated through many different mediums. Their universality makes them communicable in different parts of the world through artistic media involving, for example, music, sound and images as well as via mass media and social media more broadly (e.g., Benjaminsen 2021; Büscher 2021; Cameron et al. 2022; Chouliaraki 2013; Chouliaraki & Vestergaard 2022; Richey & Ponte 2011).

Exemplified by the SDG framework, metanarratives are also constitutive in defining what can be imagined as possible and impossible, and thus setting a discursive framework of action. According to the economists Sakiko Fukuda-Parr and Desmond McNeill, powerful nations and institutions have used their position to influence the SDG framework to support a narrative that describes challenges and social problems in a way that "points to certain types of response as obvious, and others as irrelevant or unthinkable" (2019, p. 8). In this way, they indirectly influence how less powerful countries and institutions formulate their policy agendas and program objectives (Fukuda-Parr & McNeill 2019). Similarly, it has been argued that at the country level, political discourses of climate change have been employed to hide other political agendas and defend contentious policies (Kothari 2014, p. 130; Lindegaard 2020).

Narratives, Actors and Agency

Scholarly works that aim to deconstruct discourse, including the role of narratives, are an important component of critical development studies, critical adaptation studies and political ecology. There has, however, been some concern with discourse analysis when it is based purely on written texts (Bebbington et al. 2004; Olivier de Sardan 2005). This can be problematic because "the emphasis of this work is on deconstructing the modes of discursive power than on discovering how discourse operates" (Bebbington et al. 2004, p. 37). One way that discourses operate is by being enacted through the narrative performance of stories. Even when reading official documents, it is necessary to look beyond the written text and consider documents as products of political and social processes, and thereby analyze them as having social effects and a "performative quality" (Mosse 2011, p. 12; see also Green 2011). Such social processes have been highlighted in relation to the UN Intergovernmental Panel on Climate Change (the IPCC) (Howe 2014), the SDGs (Scheyvens et al. 2016) and donor institutions' use of concepts such as "resilience" (Olwig 2009). Different actors that are part of these social processes have an important but variable impact on how narratives on development, sustainability and climate change are mediated throughout the world and eventually translated into policy and practice.

Scholars have studied how actors such as celebrity activists, diaspora alliances, "voluntourists," civil servants, philanthropists and other elites uphold, promote and challenge metanarratives (e.g., Brockington 2009; Budabin & Richey 2018, 2021; Fadlalla 2019; Funder & Mweemba 2019; Igoe 2017; Mostafanezhad 2014). A narrative's effectiveness is influenced by people's emotional and social habitus, which can lead to competing narratives among different actors. Anthropologist Amal Hassan Fadlalla, for example, analyzes competing narratives on the conflicts in Darfur and South Sudan, describing how transnational human rights and humanitarian groups emphasize a narrative of gender violence and ethnic suffering, which clashes with the narratives of "other activists fighting against the monolithic vision of the Islamist regime" (2019, p. 5). She explains that these other activists, including secular activists, "have contested and rearticulated these narratives differently to highlight their own marginal positions as political opponents in the Sudan and as exiled migrants seeking safe transnational abodes" (Fadlalla 2019, p. 5). Another example could be in relation to climate change. Focusing on the climate skepticism narrative, policy theorist Raul P. Lejano and applied linguist Shondel J. Nero show how a large subset of the US population "is taking a position on a matter of science that runs counter to the strongly held position of most of the scientific community" (2020, p. 4). In their detailed analysis of how the climate skepticism narrative has become competitive among this part of the population, they point to several factors, including that accepting climate science would also mean accepting that their lifestyle is problematic (Lejano & Nero 2020, p. 11).

Research on actors working at donor agencies, such as World Bank staff, has shown how they negotiate and bargain, but also how little agency some of them experience when formulating general policies, documents and frameworks, because overarching metanarratives, structures and interests can make it impossible for them to apply their expertise (Goldman 2005; Mosse 2011; Olwig 2009). Local practitioners who develop, implement and report on concrete projects related to development, sustainability and climate change have been conceptualized as brokers between international donors and local recipients. It has been shown how they as brokers must be fluent in universalistic development language and rationalities, so that they can translate these into meaningful projects in particular places, and vice versa (Bierschenk et al. 2002; Mosse & Lewis 2006; Olivier de Sardan 2005; Rossi 2006). Some practitioners express outright frustration with problematic development metanarratives (Maren 1997). Some actively propagate the metanarratives in the belief that it is a good communication/fundraising strategy. Yet others have become so immersed in the development rationalities that they are unaware that they are perpetuating universalistic and potentially misleading metanarratives (Olwig 2013). In these cases, the universalistic development rationalities have become part of the local development practitioners' unconscious habitus. This impacts their agency, but it does not mean that hegemonizing development metanarratives determine how they act or what they think in all situations. Rather, they operate with a simultaneity of universalistic and local rationalities, drawing on these different rationalities depending on the situation (Olwig 2013; Rossi 2006).

Development metanarratives similarly impact the practices and understandings of local recipients (Olwig 2012), but local recipients also exhibit agency. Even when they find projects to be ill-conceived, they can often find ways to use the projects to build useful social relations and gain access to resources, skills and knowledge (e.g., Nielsen 2010; Nielsen et al. 2012; Olwig & Gough 2013; Pigg 1992; Sørensen 2008). This is part of what anthropologist Olivier de Sardan refers to as the "revenge of contexts," whereby local contexts (including actors) transform the intended impact of interventions (Olivier de Sardan 2021). The agency of actors at all levels of the development sector are thus impacted by various overarching narratives, yet they can find ways of maneuvering within this narrative space. This can be illustrated by returning to the example of flooding in northern Ghana and the problem of clashing global and local views on vulnerability. In line with the globalized world view that women are the most vulnerable to disasters, local practitioners would create women's groups, and local recipients would participate in these groups. Yet, local practitioners and recipients took for granted that men would also be part of these women's groups. And, in doing so, they maneuvered within the overarching narrative space by locally redefining women's groups as groups with men as well as women (Olwig 2013).

Studying Narratives in Lived Contexts

To study the role of narratives, I have combined traditional ethnographic field methods with newer approaches. I did fieldwork amongst the people who are the object of "development" as well as those who are doing the "developing." Data collection thus involved "studying up, down and sideways" in terms of power relations (Nader 1972). With respect to research on development, sustainability and climate change, this means studying actors at different (power) levels, that is not just the recipients but also other actors such as practitioners, donors, scientists, people working for or owning for-profits and government employees. This can be called multi-level fieldwork and it included, in addition to interviews with different actor-categories, multi-level participant observation such as frequenting specific eateries, staying in different types of accommodations and using varying forms of transportation depending on which actor I was engaging with (see Figure 2).

Fieldwork was conducted over a fifteen-year period in Asia, Africa, North America and Europe, and I have thus employed a multi-sited approach. Multi-sited approaches establish the scope of research by following, for example, people, things and stories moving through different sites (Marcus 1995). In my case, these sites have involved material geographical sites as well as online sites and temporal sites in the form of events. I have found myself striking a "superhero"-pose at a sustainability workshop for businesspeople in a fancy hotel in Copenhagen, Denmark; I have sat in the shade of a baobab tree in

Figure 2 Multi-level fieldwork can involve "multi-level" forms of transportation. When I was doing fieldwork with local practitioners, I would ride with them in their donor-sponsored four-wheel drives. When doing fieldwork with local recipients, however, I would always take my bicycle, as shown in this photograph. Ghana, December 2009.

northern Ghana as part of a community meeting organized by local practitioners who were introducing the concept of vulnerability; and I have drunk copious amounts of strong green tea in Vietnamese coastal villages while listening to villagers explain the benefits and challenges of flooding. This approach has been adopted because narratives do not just take the form of texts, they are told orally, performed (or enacted) and practiced in substantive contexts. Multi-sited, multi-level ethnographic approaches are therefore important in research on narratives of development, sustainability and climate change (see also, Krauss 2009; Li 2007). Multi-level methods can facilitate the understanding of lived experiences among different actor categories, while multi-sited research can illuminate both how hegemonizing metanarratives gain their authority worldwide by traveling between sites and how different actor categories at the different sites respond to and are impacted by these narratives.

The fieldwork took place in countries that provide aid as well as those that receive aid. Denmark has for many years been one of the largest donors by percentage of gross national income, while the USA has been the largest donor by dollar amount. Vietnam, Ghana and Tanzania are all countries that have received a significant amount of aid from both the USA and Denmark, with Tanzania, for example, being the country that has received the most development assistance from Denmark. Importantly, fieldwork has furthermore taken place in countries with differing histories, religions, governance systems and economies. For example, in relation to governance, Vietnam is a communist one-party state while Ghana is a multiparty democracy. Tanzania was a one-party socialist state for about thirty years after independence, and is today a multiparty democracy. By including this variety of sites, it is possible to examine how remarkably similar hegemonizing narratives of development, sustainability and climate change show up in many different contexts, and how the actors in these varying contexts challenge and maneuver within, or even perpetuate, these narratives in differing ways. Yet, while I focus on particular sites in Vietnam, Ghana, Tanzania, the USA and Denmark, where the environmental and societal contexts vary, these study sites are nevertheless interconnected through the international development sector, and therefore have in common that they are part of what the anthropologist Raymond Apthorpe has described as "Aidland." Apthorpe writes that Aidland has: "its own mental topographies, languages of discourse, lore and custom, and approaches to organizational knowledge and learning" (Apthorpe 2011, p. 199). The multiple sites where I have done fieldwork can be considered to all be part of this Aidland, and as such, my fieldwork has in some ways taken place in one extended field site (c.f. Olwig 2007) comprised of many different geographical locations.

By following influential metanarratives of development, sustainability and climate change as they move among different actor categories between varying places in the extended international field site of the development sector, it became possible to identify narrative structures and elements and how they evolved, while central features nevertheless remained the same. *A Bit Too Simple* thereby engages simultaneously with narratives and their movements and with actors and their relations. Using narratives as its analytical lens and drawing on theories from critical development studies, critical adaptation studies and political ecology, it illuminates how metanarratives circulate and become interrelated, what makes them powerful and for whom, and why and to what effect they are told.

Setting the Scene: Narrative Elements, Ethnographic Cases and Multiple Sites

Each of the four ethnographic sections takes place in different sites and focuses on one of the following narrative elements: the crisis, the main characters, the solution and emerging storylines. The sections describe, exemplify and analyze different, yet converging, metanarratives, counterposing them to actors' concrete lived experiences in the field. Taken together, they reveal absurdities, tragedies and sometimes agency in the face of hegemony.

Section 2, "Crisis, A Call to Action: The Making of Floods into Disasters," takes place in Vietnam and investigates the characteristics of an oversimplified "crisis storyline" and its consequences. Taking a point of departure in an empirical case of floods in Vietnam, it shows how a crisis storyline reduced a complex system of endemic flooding into a disaster caused by external climate change. Conveniently for the government, this simplified crisis storyline could be used to downplay the local political dimensions of environmental issues while for development actors it served as a call to action. Vietnam is one of the countries that is most vulnerable to climate change, but periodic floods are known locally to be a beneficial part of the socio-ecological system. Thus, while some floods in Vietnam certainly are disastrous, this should not imply that floods in general are disastrous. Floods can happen quickly and seem dramatic, explaining why external actors, such as donors, easily may perceive them generally as disasters. Moreover, flooding as a negative event has been an important narrative element in many mythical and religious narratives from different parts of the world, where a flood is presented as a form of divine punishment. The storyline in which floods are dangerous and of apocalyptic dimensions is thus familiar to many, making for a convincing narrative.

By looking specifically at the crisis storyline, Section 2 lays the basis for the remaining sections, and for the overall argument of the Element. It demonstrates that a crisis of disastrous dimensions can work as an effective narrative tool. The crisis functions as a call to action for the hero and creates a sense of urgency. This can result in the normal processes of critical scrutiny and accountability being skipped in the interest of time. In the following sections, new narrative elements are introduced, but the overall narrative storyline remains one of simplified crisis as an important call to action for the hero. I argue that, to a great extent, it is this shared simplified crisis storyline that enables the converging of development hero metanarratives with other influential sustainability and climate change metanarratives.

Section 3, "Villains, Victims and Heroes: The Cast of Characters and Their Roles in Environmental Decline," is based on multi-sited fieldwork in northern Ghana, the USA and Denmark, and introduces the characters of "the villain, the victim and the hero." There has been a long history of villainizing human behavior in relation to the environment. This can be linked to ancient religious narratives that entail a "declensionist" plot of human destructive behavior and decline (or declension) leading to the demise of nature (Merchant 2013). Declensionist narratives mandate that it is necessary to recover an imagined (and unattainable) lost ideal, Edenic, natural state to be saved from an imminent crisis. Many contemporary environmental narratives can be seen to use similar tropes, thus linking to familiar, deep-rooted patterns of thinking that have spread to the rest of the world through Western imperial expansion, colonialism and missionary activity. As a result of this process, blaming human behavior for crisis, even when this is not warranted, is especially prevalent in relation to populations in the Global South. The section's case draws on the example of desertification in northern Ghana, in a semi-arid region that has a long history of interaction with the international development sector, and therefore also of development metanarratives. Desertification is part of large-scale environmental processes, but in what is referred to as the desertification narrative, policymakers, donors, practitioners and even local communities attribute desertification to local populations' presumed irresponsible ("villainous") use of the environment, thereby justifying ("heroic") external intervention. Thus, even though the desertification narrative has been criticized in scientific research, it still shows up as a metanarrative across several different contexts (Herrmann & Hutchinson 2005; Leach & Mearns 1996; Roe 1991).

The object of Section 3 is to present the different characters of villain, victim and hero, and the part they play in development hero metanarratives. These figures are key to understanding why certain narratives, such as the desertification narrative, are reproduced by differing institutions and actors. The hegemonizing nature of narratives such as the desertification narrative can result in local populations internalizing a role as ignorant villains and helpless victims, and likewise associating first missionaries and then also development practitioners with heroic saviorism. Such narratives can thus negatively affect how local people imagine and understand both their environmental challenges and their ability to develop constructive solutions, while also justifying interventions and potentially problematic solutions by external development actors.

Section 4, "Solutions: How Trees Became the Answer to Climate Change," moves to southern Tanzania and southern Ghana and focuses on the narrative element of the "solution." The section examines how an underlying oversimplified crisis storyline can foster problematic climate change solutions and actions. In these solutions, we furthermore again see links to long-standing religious and development hero metanarratives of decline and environmental destruction – the narratives are converging. To enable universalistic solutions, climate change is often oversimplified and the problem of an excess of CO_2 in the atmosphere is singled out. This leads to interventions that emphasize reduced carbon emissions, carbon credits and carbon sequestration (often through forestry) – solutions that are universally quantifiable and measurable. Carbon credits allow actors with resources, such as countries, organizations, businesses or even individual consumers, to purchase what in a religious context would be termed "indulgences" for the absolution of their carbon sins. Yet, major carbon sequestration initiatives revolve around (CO_2 absorbing) forests *only* in the Global South – for example, the UN initiative Reduced Emissions for Deforestation and Forest Degradation (REDD+) – and include external actors as facilitators. Such initiatives are framed as incentivizing communities to rectify local forest mismanagement. A familiar problematic narrative emerges here – the ostensible villains/victims in the Global South need to change how they manage nature (trees) to avoid decline, and the heroic external actors, largely from the Global North, provide the incentives and knowledge to do this. This section synthesizes findings from collaborative mixed-method research projects in Tanzania and Ghana that investigated different types of external interventions focused on tree planting. Examining the rationales behind, and the consequences of, these interventions, the section shows that even though trees are CO_2 absorbing, tree planting can be problematic if the complex role of trees in the socioeconomic and ecological landscape is not sufficiently considered. Tree planting can be highly beneficial, but undifferentiated and monocrop tree planting can negatively impact the environment and people's socioeconomic conditions.

By examining the narrative element of the solution, Section 4 shows how the familiar narrative elements discussed in the previous sections – a storyline revolving around an oversimplified crisis, a declensionist plot and a cast of characters that includes villains, victims and heroes – can end up justifying problematic tree planting initiatives in the Global South. Carbon credit initiatives, for example, that result in monocrop tree planting in the Global South not only have questionable environmental outcomes, they also negatively impact the lives of people in the Global South. In the Global North, on the other hand, carbon credits make it possible to basically continue doing business-as-usual. This solution is thus not particularly efficient or equitable, but rather one that challenges the geopolitical status quo the least.

Section 5, "For-Profit Characters and Storylines: Sustainability Superheroes and Profitable Redemption," identifies and explores for-profit hero metanarratives that have emerged in the era of the SDGs, focusing on Denmark, a frontrunner SDG country. The SDGs were considered a game changer because they, as opposed to the previous UN Millennium Development Goals (MDGs), applied to the whole world, not just the Global South. Moreover, they identified for-profits as key stakeholders. The importance of for-profits as a funding mechanism for the SDGs significantly magnified the role of businesses and consultancies, thereby enabling them to influence how the SDGs would be addressed. As a result, narratives emerged that justified combining profit-making with "doing good," while encouraging what could be called profitable redemption. Doing good was understood as an action that could be considered to contribute to reaching the SDGs – thereby merging issues related to development, sustainability and climate change. Based on event ethnography focused on businesses and doing good, this section shows that these for-profit hero metanarratives, as with long-standing development hero metanarratives, continued to revolve around a crisis and included heroes and villains, but generally focused less on the victims. The villain category also continued to include local people engaging in what is perceived to be problematic practices. However, the for-profit hero metanarratives further developed the figure of the hero by casting anyone, anywhere, as potential "sustainability superheroes" who can do good by, for example, paying a for-profit to plant a tree or purchasing a product made from recycled materials. These superheroes may feel good by doing good, but their actions arguably have limited effect on development, sustainability and climate change, and gloss over the historical-geographical structures that perpetuate inequality.

By analyzing for-profit hero metanarratives, this section shows which narrative elements changed and which remained the same, and the consequences thereof for understandings and practices of development, sustainability and climate change. The section argues that one of the key reasons why these for-profit hero metanarratives have become forceful is that the SDGs reduced sustainable development to universalistic goals and targets that could be addressed through business-like management, whether by for-profits, non-profits or governments. Sustainable development was thereby described in abstract global terms, reflected through simplified, seemingly apolitical indicators that are measurable, quantifiable and, not least, monetizable.

Section 6, "Conclusion: Mobilizing Grounded Stories," focuses on the need to mobilize a multiplicity of grounded stories to nuance globalized metanarratives. By bringing together the previous sections, it shows that examining the simplified crisis storylines, the interrelated characters of the victim, villain and hero, and the solutions the storylines generate provides an understanding of how globalized metanarratives converge. They do so in part by simplifying complexity, standardizing storylines and typecasting characters to appear generically familiar, while the solutions tend to support the geopolitical status quo. Such metanarratives are problematic because they gloss over, and even reinforce, inequalities through a simplification that streamlines challenges so that they can be discussed, addressed and measured at an abstract global level and across sectors and disciplinary divides, while overlooking lived realities. The section posits that by bringing to light, and critically analyzing, these dominating globalized metanarratives, it is possible to challenge them constructively and thereby formulate and implement more effective and equitable policy and practice. Problems arise especially when hegemonizing metanarratives are globally elevated to conventional wisdom.

The Element concludes by pointing to the importance of not only challenging these wisdoms, but also actively seeking out other more grounded stories. By paying attention to stories emerging from the particular experiences of a broader range of actors, such as is done in this Element, solutions can build on a wider knowledge base that is grounded in lived realities with which citizens can identify. Such solutions thereby can potentially mobilize local agency rather than global fantasy.

2 Crisis, A Call to Action: The Making of Floods into Disasters

> *This year there has been no flood, which has many consequences. The first one is many mice and insects damaging the farming production. And in this village, we have another way of earning money, that is fishing. When there is no flood, it is quite hard, we cannot fish much, so we cannot earn much.*
>
> (Village level leader, author interview, central Vietnam, January 2015)

> *... reducing vulnerability to floods is not the same as stopping floods ... [F]lood prevention will produce its own set of victims: those who are going to be made worse off by the proposed projects. It is even possible that more people will suffer longer-term damage to their livelihoods.*
>
> (Wisner et al. 2004, pp. 195, 197)

In 2014, I joined a development-funded research project that was focused on increasing resilience and reducing vulnerability to climate change–induced water disasters, especially climate-induced flooding, in three provinces in central Vietnam. An important component of the project was to provide Vietnamese local administrators with an interactive digital map that would make data generated by the project easily accessible – what was described as a Participatory Geographical Information System (PGIS). The project had been ongoing since 2012, and was funded by a development research collaboration grant from Denmark's development cooperation, Danida (formerly the Danish International Development Agency). The project was based in Hanoi and led by a Vietnamese university, with a Danish university as a collaborative research partner. As a human geographer who has worked with Geographical Information Systems (GIS) as a practitioner and as a researcher, my role in the project was to examine, from a GIS-informed social science perspective, the local stakeholders' experiences of climate change, but also the PGIS. I collected data through embedded participant observation of the Vietnamese research project as a participant-insider, what is known as "insider ethnography" (Mosse 2006), and through interviews with villagers, village leaders and local administrators from the project's study sites.

Vietnam is severely affected by climate change. But contrary to the project's emphasis on problematic climate-induced flooding, many interviewees were concerned that there had been no floods during the year of 2014. A year without flooding was considered highly unusual, and several stated they had never experienced this before. Furthermore, local residents emphasized how government-initiated environmental interventions (e.g., dams), rather than climate change, had problematically changed the nature of the local flooding that is necessary and beneficial for farming practices and fishing (see Figure 3). It quickly became apparent in these interviews, as well as through discussions with the other researchers in the project, that there was a disconnect between specific local experiences and oversimplified globally circulating, hegemonizing crisis storylines that presented all floods as disastrous and all environmental challenges as being linked to climate change.

As outlined in the Introduction, the crisis storyline in development hero metanarratives includes an imagined idealized normal that is disrupted by a crisis that serves as a call to action for the heroic development practitioner. In Vietnam, flooding has been used as an entry point for a simplifying crisis storyline. But to properly fit this crisis storyline, an idealized "normal" is imagined in which floods in Vietnam are unnatural, and flooding events therefore constitute the disruptive crisis – the call to action. Attributing the seasonal flooding that has been endemic to the area to a new type of disaster caused by

Figure 3 Fishing, using for example fish nets, as seen in this picture, is important to local livelihoods. According to the local population, seasonal flooding improves fishing. Vietnam, May 2014.
Photo by author.

climate change aids this reimagining of floods. Floods as crisis function as a dramatic narrative element in several ancient, mythical stories, and because of the scale and suddenness of many floods, they are often treated as an apocalyptic "act of God." An example is the story recounted in the Biblical book of Genesis, where God is punishing people for their sins. As this section will show, however, the simplified storyline of flooding as crisis does not capture the full complexity of environmental challenges and flooding adequately in the context of Vietnam. While flooding does cause damage, the complete absence of floods can be equally damaging, as is also illustrated by the introductory quotes. Yet, research shows a tendency to underestimate, or even ignore, floods' benefits in flood management planning (Tran et al. 2008, p. 120).

Instrumentalizing Climate Change

Densely populated deltas are expected to see a rise in the number and intensity of flooding events (Tran & Rodela 2019) and the UN IPCC highlights Vietnam as being one of the most vulnerable countries to climate change (IPCC 2022). As a result, Vietnam is among the countries that receive the highest levels of climate-related development finance (Gverdtsiteli 2023). Climate-related funding became available at a time when Vietnam experienced a decline in foreign aid as the country had advanced to middle-income country status (Bruun 2012). While increased national governmental attention and external economic support to address climate change are crucial considering the severity of climate change impacts, research has found that the Vietnamese state and external actors alike strategically use a focus on climate change for other purposes as well.

After Japan and the World Bank, Germany has during the past decade given the highest amount of climate-related development support to Vietnam. Research has shown how this finance has been used to deepen political and economic ties between the two countries (Gverdtsiteli 2023, p. 36). Additionally, donors have been shown to emphasize the negative impacts of climate change in situations where climate change may not be the pressing issue. Organizations like the World Bank and the Asian Development Bank have stressed, for example, how the impact of climate change on rice production would affect rural populations dependent on agriculture in the coastal areas of central Vietnam. However, they failed to mention that many of these areas had already moved away from a sole focus on rice production. Urbanization, tourism, shrimp farming and construction projects that are linked to government policies that explicitly further industrialization have all reduced the economic importance of agriculture to the local population in these areas (Bruun 2012).

Similarly, research on the discursive production of climate subjects in Vietnam has illuminated how global climate change discourse and knowledge have been appropriated by Vietnamese policymakers, who have used climate change as a tool not only to ensure continued funding, but also "to project cohesion with powerful international actors" (Lindegaard 2020, p. 165; Zink 2013). Additionally, the Vietnamese state has been shown to reframe political interventions as related to climate change in order to legitimize contentious interventions and further social control (Gverdtsiteli 2023; Lindegaard 2020).[4] This includes, for example, relocating populations to further urbanization but calling the relocation a flood protection measure.

As discussed earlier, the narratives that gain currency and become metanarratives are often the ones that are aligned with powerful actors' interests. In the case of flooding in Vietnam, these actors include the development sector as well as the state. When common environmental processes, such as seasonal flooding, are reframed as exceptional and part of climate-induced processes, issues linked to local structural inequalities, poor governance and deeply rooted

---

[4] As discussed in the Introduction, such acts can be considered a form of "revenge of contexts" (cf. Olivier de Sardan 2021), whereby actors, in this case state actors, display agency by using international interventions and aid for different ends than intended.

vulnerabilities are more easily decentered (Bankoff et al. 2004; Mikulewicz 2020; Wisner et al. 2004). This is in part because during periods of crisis, time is regarded as being of the essence, and immediate political action deemed necessary (Mosurska et al. 2023; Paprocki 2018). This can limit the recognition of the need to pay attention to locally grounded stories and for the critical interrogation of contested political pathways (Arnall et al. 2014; Arnall & Kothari 2015; Castree et al. 2014). Instrumentalizing the serious issue of climate change in this way is problematic, not least because important and necessary climate change funds can wind up being misused.

Based on my interviews, I will in the following give examples of state-led infrastructural and construction projects that were destructive in relation to seasonal flooding, thereby challenging the simplified crisis storyline on global climate change-induced flooding.

Moving State-Led Infrastructural and Construction Projects Away from the Spotlight

Several interviewees related how different government-initiated local construction projects had a major impact on how water flowed and was trapped. These projects could be problematic because they, among other things, caused water to move too quickly or to flow into abnormal places. Examples of such projects included sand mining and infrastructure development (e.g., roads and canals):

> *Firstly, about the drainage system, some infrastructure and some buildings were constructed, but the drainage was not developed accordingly to serve the development of this infrastructure. So, the drainage does not have enough capacity and will cause local flooding in some areas in some regions.* (Communal level local administrator, author interview, central Vietnam, January 2015)

Interviews also highlighted that forest management upstream affected how the water flowed. In one of the study sites, interviewees explained that whereas flooding formerly began several days after the first uphill precipitation, now only one day would pass before the flooding started. They attributed this to deforestation. Forest management is a highly complex and contentious issue, as it concerns not just the size of the forest, but also the type of forest covering the land. Areas of old growth forest are increasingly being cut and converted to more commercially profitable state-supported forest plantations and, in addition, illegal large-scale logging is prevalent (Bruun 2012). Research has shown, furthermore: "that it is often the management activities associated with forestry, [such as] cultivation, drainage or road construction, rather than the presence or absence of forests themselves ... [that] influence the size and frequency of floods" (Tran et al. 2010, p. 2187). The government, reflecting classic technocratic high-modernist ideology (cf. Scott 1998), instead blamed shifting cultivation, thereby justifying its attempts to eliminate this long-standing practice amongst the upstream ethnic minority groups (Tran et al. 2010, p. 2196, see also Section 4). Yet, these small-scale agroforestry systems traditionally included practices that ameliorated damaging flooding.

Another government-initiated environmental intervention that altered water flows in problematic ways, according to interviewees, was the establishment of shrimp and crab farms. These were encouraged by the government as a means of livelihood diversification (Bruun & Olwig 2015). Shrimp and crab farms are very vulnerable to forceful flooding, because all the shrimp and crabs can easily be lost. Furthermore, these farms offer no means of absorbing or slowing the water flows, quite to the contrary (Bruun 2012; Bruun & Olwig 2015). Such farms sometimes replace wetland habitats and coastal mangrove forests that serve many important functions, including as buffer areas between the ocean and habitation. This was, for example, the case in India during the 2004 Indian Ocean Tsunami (Danielsen et al. 2005; Olwig et al. 2007). Though the wetland habitats and coastal mangrove forests are open to flooding from the sea, they also break the speed of flooding, thereby moderating its effect, while at the same time providing ecological support for maritime resources like wild fish, for which flooding can be positive. Nevertheless, the conversion of wetlands and mangroves into shrimp and crab farms, along with other factors such as the expansion of the built environment, are common in the area.

Interviewees also noted that hydropower plants and irrigation reservoirs caused two major problems locally: 1) flooding was aggravated because water must be released from the dams during heavy rain to prevent them from bursting; and 2) dams stored and diverted water so that less water reached downstream outside the flooding season. In addition to the issues raised by the interviewees, research has also linked the building of hydropower plants to the forced migration of ethnic minorities; forest destruction; water pollution; negative effects on the ability of fish to migrate and spawn; disruption of the natural hydrological flows and sediment transport; and to damaging changes in river flows and ecological systems upstream and downstream (Bruun 2012; Green & Baird 2020). It is difficult, however, to study the impact of hydropower plants in Vietnam because "data on the full scale of these operations are not publicly available (and not all operations are registered)" (Bruun 2012, p. 258). As hydropower plants are a contentious issue in Vietnam, it is simply not in the interest of the government that these data be accessible. As illustrated by these examples, the interviewees highlighted multiple causes of problematic flooding that had little to do with climate change. They also challenged the simplified crisis storyline in relation to flood as crisis.

Can Flooding Be Both Good and Bad?

"Water is synonymous with life and culture in Southeast Asia" (Miller 2018, p. 285). The importance of water is marked through various water festivals and other water-related activities. In Vietnam, for example, water puppetry is an ancient tradition that originally took place in flooded rice paddies. This does not mean that floods and typhoons cannot cause major damage, especially when they occur in tandem. In fact, a common term used by my interviewees instead of disaster was "bão lũ," which simply combines the terms for flood and typhoon. Floods are thus linked to life, culture, potential disaster and to important livelihood activities (see Figure 4). A lack of flooding can, for example, destroy farm production and minimize fishing activities, as explained by the village leader quoted earlier.

Even though water and flooding are integral to Vietnamese farming practices, with the influx of simplified crisis storylines and an instrumentalization of climate change, flooding is being recast negatively. During interviews, for

Figure 4 Flooding is useful for rice cultivation, as seen here, and many other livelihood activities, such as the raising of ducks. Vietnam, December 2014. Photo by author.

example, one of my Vietnamese interpreters, whose full-time job was at an international NGO concerned with climate change, habitually translated "experience floods" to "suffer from floods," even when the interviewee was explaining the benefits of floods, as in the example below:

> *When there is a flood, the fish and the shrimp and other kinds of seafood flow into this area and we can fish a lot, and also the fish from the sea, we can fish. But now no flood, so the amount is less. And nearly every year this area suffers from [experiences] flood. When at its lowest it just reaches the road and in 2010 when it was at the highest there was one meter of water ... [in] the house, I had to move to this area under the roof. We really like floods, because we can fish and the farming production is very good. No flooding affects our health, fishing and farming production.* (Village level leader, author interview, central Vietnam, January 2015)

While this quote overall shows that the village leader was happy about floods, it also demonstrates that floods do lead to situations that, for an outsider, could appear disastrous – such as having a meter of water in the house. But the area under the roof that the village leader moved to, when the water was at its highest, was constructed exactly for this purpose. It is a common feature of houses in many places where flooding is a regular and important part of the ecosystem. The need for such an area may seem inconvenient. Yet, to give a parallel example, snow can also be inconvenient, and therefore it is also part of everyday life in many areas of the world to use a snowplow after heavy snowfall. And even though floods and snowstorms can be deadly, it is an oversimplification to categorize every snowstorm and flood as a disaster just because they can be inconvenient. To the contrary, many people in the far north depend on winter snow as a reservoir of water and as an infrastructure for traveling by sledge, snowmobile and ski. Likewise, floods, as has been seen, can be very important. Yet, this complexity is lost in oversimplified crisis storylines, such as the storylines that are typical of development hero metanarratives.

This section has introduced the simplified crisis storyline in development hero metanarratives. It has described the potential problematic consequences of such simplification for understandings of local social, political and ecological complexity, using the example of seasonal flooding in Vietnam. Various metanarratives of development, sustainability and climate change often share this simplified crisis element as a call to action. This, in part, is what makes it possible for them to converge, as will be further elaborated in the following sections. Using the example of the desertification narrative, Section 3 will introduce the figures of the victim, the villain and the hero, who are important characters in the crisis storyline of development hero metanarratives.

3 Villains, Victims and Heroes: The Cast of Characters and Their Roles in Environmental Decline

Climate change affects the weather, for instance when cutting down the trees. The trees help the rainfall, when there is rainfall the weather is wet and cool ...
[Where did you hear that the trees will affect the rainfall?]
I have heard a lot about that from all the [nongovernmental and governmental] organizations that I mentioned that work here, they tell us the importance of growing trees. We have therefore formed a committee to protect trees, it will go and find out why you are cutting a tree and arrest you.
(Farmer, author interview, northern Ghana, March 2010)

In the 2000s, West Africa experienced unusually heavy and persistent rains that caused extensive flooding. The flooding's extraordinary severity was seen to indicate a changing climate. I did fieldwork in northern Ghana in 2009–2010 as part of my multi-sited research on the changes taking place in the development sector because of the increased concern with climate change. This included participant observation among and interviews with donors in Copenhagen, Denmark, Washington, DC, and New York City in the USA, and in Ghana among practitioners and recipients in Accra, Tamale and smaller communities in the semi-arid Upper East Region, including in its regional capital Bolgatanga. During fieldwork in the Upper East Region, the evidence of destruction from flooding was dramatically visible. When conducting my interviews, however, I found that it was very difficult to engage people in conversations about flooding. There was instead a preoccupation with insufficient rains, linked to an overarching metanarrative, the desertification narrative, that has dominated perceptions of the Sahel and drylands of West Africa, and the resultant development interventions. The desertification narrative, which effectively blames local resource mismanagement for causing droughts and desertification, gained considerable ground during the great Sahelian droughts of the 1970s and 1980s. Despite repeated scientific critique, this explanation of drought continues to be a prevalent environmental narrative (Herrmann & Hutchinson 2005; Leach & Mearns 1996; Marcussen 1999; Tschakert et al. 2010). Thus, even though too much rain leading to flooding had caused substantial damage when I did my fieldwork, donors, development practitioners and the local population repeatedly reverted to the desertification narrative by emphasizing the absence of rain and the need to improve rainfall by rectifying local resource mismanagement such as tree cutting.

In this section, I will use the case of the desertification narrative in northern Ghana to introduce the figures of the victims, the villains and the heroes that are typically included in development hero metanarratives. In the desertification narrative, the local population – the development recipients – are portrayed as both the unwitting "villains" and the helpless "victims," having degraded their own environment. Development practitioners and donors, on the other hand, are presented as the "heroes" who will save the environment as well as the livelihoods of the victims/aid recipients by making them aware of what is deemed local problematic behavior and how to fix it. By emphasizing local resource mismanagement, external interventions are justified. But the broader and external drivers of environmental challenges remain unaddressed, while the local people are taught that their approach to and understanding of environmental challenges is inappropriate. This can lead to a sense of apathy and dependency on external interventions.

On Villains, Victims and Heroes

Nongovernmental and donor organizations in the development sector must communicate their work to potential funders. An important audience, or spectator, in this regard is the public in the Global North that through taxes, purchases or direct donations in part fund their work. In this communication, the popular storyline characters of the villain, victim and hero can be an important component (Ascough 2018; Budabin & Richey 2018). The villain in the storyline is presented as engaging in "villainous behavior" that takes the form of, for example, "poor governance" or "problematic local cultural practices." In the case of the desertification narrative, the villainous behavior is destructive land-use practices. The victim is usually the local population in the Global South that can be described as the "distant other," that is, someone the spectator "does not experientially or culturally identify with and cannot, in principle, share the misfortune of" (Chouliaraki 2006, p. 22). This distant other is frequently portrayed as vulnerable and suffering, and in need of help (Chouliaraki & Vestergaard 2022).

The hero in the desertification narrative is the NGO, or other external development agent, who in relation to the spectator also functions as what anthropologist Jim Igoe calls the expert-interlocutor, "one to whom the viewer can relate, but who still possesses sufficient authority to instill meaning and order on what might otherwise appear frighteningly chaotic" (Igoe 2017, p. 27). Sometimes these expert-interlocutors are replaced by celebrity-heroes who work as NGO "ambassadors" to draw attention to a cause, bear witness to a difficult-to-access situation and thereby mediate (and thus also control) the distant viewer's experience and understanding of the issues at stake (Budabin & Richey 2018; Igoe 2017; Kapoor 2013; Mostafanezhad 2013; Richey & Brockington 2020).

The categories of the villain, victim and hero as cast in development hero metanarratives have been criticized for being problematic for several reasons. One reason is that they disempower and deny the agency of local populations. As journalist Michael Maren explains, "it is in their helplessness that they become a marketable commodity" (Maren 1997, p. 3). In the words of a frustrated Save the Children staffer quoted by Maren: "The message of all our advertising at Save was that Africans are too stupid to take care of themselves. And if we don't do it, their parents and their governments aren't responsible enough to do it" (Maren 1997, p. 157). As this quote indicates, the staff at an NGO does not necessarily agree with, and may even be horrified by, the use of such tropes. Another, and closely related, problem is that these development hero metanarratives include just the right amount of misery to support political and fundraising strategies without highlighting the role of the spectator in causing the misery in the first place (Igoe 2017, p. 23). These metanarratives thereby gloss over that the development sector to some degree is rooted in, and continues to operate within, historically unequal North–South power relations and colonial legacies (Kapoor 2008; Kothari 2019).

While this Element focuses on particular dominant development hero metanarratives, narrative variations and competing narratives of course also exist. Nongovernmental organizations tweak and vary their narratives according to their mandate. Thus, advocacy organizations, such as those focusing on climate justice, "would want to personify strength, resistance, and solidarity" (Pruce 2016, p. 65). Humanitarian NGOs, on the other hand, "would desire a less antagonistic frame by evoking empathy and compassion. Drawing on emotional narratives of helplessness, the needy subject requires charitable assistance from affluent viewers" (Pruce 2016, p. 65). The human rights movements, according to legal scholar Makau wa Mutua, often invoke narratives where victims are described "as hordes of nameless, despairing, and dispirited masses" (Mutua 2001, p. 229). Moreover, in the Global South, the state is typically given the role of the "savage," as an operational instrument of a "savage culture," enabling human rights international NGOs (the "saviors") to "concentrate their work on the violations of civil and political rights" by "savage" states (Mutua 2001, p. 216).

In recent years, as a result of the phrase "Indigenous knowledge" entering "the lexicon of development practitioners and theorists," competing narratives have emerged that place Indigenous Peoples and marginalized people not only in the role of victims, but also in the role of heroes and as actors with capacity (Agrawal 1995, p. 413). Such narratives importantly acknowledge the agency of Indigenous Peoples and marginalized people. However, there has also been a tendency to romanticize and compartmentalize Indigenous knowledge, and thereby create a "sterile dichotomy between indigenous and western" (Agrawal 1995, p. 433). Furthermore, as political scientist Arun Agrawal has pointed out, while the focus on Indigenous knowledge includes an emphasis on "'empowering' marginalized groups," there tends to be less of an emphasis on the need for "significant shifts in existing power relationships" (Agrawal 1995, p. 416). If the need for such a shift is not recognized, Indigenous and marginalized groups risk simply being inscribed in a different universalistic development metanarrative that fundamentally maintains the status quo. If marginalized groups' narratives are to have transformative power, it is necessary to consider "multiple domains and types of knowledges, with differing logics and epistemologies" (Agrawal 1995, p. 433). This will be a core topic in the Conclusion.

Returning to the development hero metanarratives, the villains, victims and hero characters, as noted earlier, easily become linked to a modern-day "civilizing" project. As part of the storyline, an NGO comes to the rescue by introducing a solution to the suffering population and the storyline concludes with the local population now happy because they have received new material resources and/or been enlightened. In the case of desertification in northern Ghana, the solution was to "civilize" the local population in relation to their management of nature. This idea is closely associated with familiar ancient religious and mythical storylines, such as the declensionist plot that informed colonial approaches to resource management, and which continue to frame many development interventions and policy documents on environmental crisis, sustainability and climate change.

Environmental Narratives: The Declensionist Plot

In the Judeo-Christian Bible, one of the most iconic and well-known storylines revolves around Adam and Eve who disobey God by eating an apple from the Tree of the Knowledge of Good and Evil. This leads God to punish them by expelling them from Eden and its ideal unspoiled nature. Having been evicted from Eden, humans are no longer part of this nature, and the idea of Eden thus plays an important role in the construction of the foundational Western modern dichotomy between nature and society. The storyline of Adam and Eve feeds into a recurring declensionist plot that emphasizes human destructive behavior leading to deteriorating nature (or decline/declension). This is also known as the "Paradise Lost" narrative (Hoben 1995; Marcussen 1999, p. 96). In order to be saved from the resulting imminent crisis, humans strive to recover this imagined (and unattainable) ideal (Merchant 2013).

The declensionist plot and the desire to "reinvent Eden" (Merchant 2013) can be linked to environmental interventions that aim to "erase" human influence.

They do so through various forms of "fortress conservation" that evict local people in the name of protecting "nature." This is done even if the local people were inhabiting their customary lands and relied on these lands for their livelihoods, such as for grazing (Brockington 2002). Such conservation problematically not only makes it difficult for local populations to maintain a livelihood. It can also inadvertently damage the ecosystems that conservation was intended to save. For example, in Denmark, an attempt to "preserve" the heaths, treasured for their beauty and their contribution to the diversity of the Danish landscape, resulted in farmers being banned from using the areas for sheep grazing and shifting cultivation. This, in turn, led to the heaths transforming into inaccessible, biologically uninteresting shrub, because grazing and shifting cultivation are key to maintaining the heath landscape (Olwig 2021 [1984]). Similarly, controlled burning as used in shifting cultivation has often been unfairly demonized and forbidden (Boserup 1965).

Trees are an important element in Eden, indeed two trees, the Tree of Life and the Tree of the Knowledge of Good and Evil, stand at its center (Merchant 2013, p. 1). Furthermore, the tree is a symbol of the fertility of nature and trees are perceived to be necessary in order to recover an ideal nature (Merchant 2013). As will be discussed further in Section 4, trees, as ideal Edenic nature, and undifferentiated tree planting are often uncritically celebrated solutions to sustainability and climate change challenges, including in the desertification narrative. While the declensionist plot is linked to ideas of conservation and wilderness preservation more generally, through missionary activities, colonialism and development interventions it has become particularly prevalent when discussing environmental challenges in the Global South. Furthermore, in the Global South, the declensionist plot is being combined with neo-Malthusian narratives that claim the problems of local resource mismanagement are compounded by overpopulation (Boserup 1965; Hoben 1995).

The long history and widespread application of the declensionist plot has in effect led to the notion that local land-use practices are to blame for environmental challenges acquiring "the status of conventional wisdom" among many development professionals (Leach & Mearns 1996, p. 1). This is well exemplified by the desertification narrative that continues to persist despite continuous and growing evidence questioning the scientific foundation of such neo-Malthusian narratives (Boserup 1965; Hoben 1995; Leach & Mearns 1996; Marcussen 1999).

The Desertification Narrative

Already in the 1920s, scientists became concerned that the Sahara Desert was expanding and making land unproductive. The cause was thought to be land mismanagement, in particular overgrazing, shifting agriculture and the shortening of agricultural fallow periods. In 1949, the term desertification began to be used when referring to this theory (Batterbury & Warren 2001). In the 1970s, meteorologist Jule Gregory Charney and colleagues used a global circulation model to show a positive feedback mechanism between decreasing plant cover and a corresponding decrease in precipitation due to increasing sunlight reflection (albedo), what became known as the Charney hypothesis. With this hypothesis, they effectively argued that anthropogenic reduction of plant life could cause drought rather than drought causing desertification (Charney et al. 1975).

Today, these explanations of drought are questioned by climate researchers (Tschakert et al. 2010). There is significant ambiguity about the nature of land degradation and desertification, and a lack of measurable criteria to document such environmental changes (Leach & Mearns 1996; Marcussen 1999; Roe 1991). Semi-arid climates "are intrinsically defined by alternating wet and dry periods on annual and decadal timescales" (Tschakert et al. 2010, p. 472). Some studies even suggest a possible recovery of rainfall and a greening of the Sahel (Fensholt et al. 2012; Herrmann et al. 2005). Nevertheless, land degradation and desertification narratives are still prevalent in policy agendas, and the general mental image of West Africa remains dominated by drought, land degradation and desertification narratives, with famine, hunger and food insecurity constituting the quintessential core (Tschakert et al. 2010). For many, it can be extremely difficult to imagine these arid and semi-arid regions in any other way – for example, as flood-prone areas (Tschakert et al. 2010).

Illustrating the power of the desertification metanarrative, geographers William G. Moseley and Paul Laris describe and reflect on their experiences as Peace Corps Volunteers in the 1980s, when they had "no apparent incentive – financial or professional – for supporting the dominant narrative" of desertification (Moseley & Laris 2008, p. 61). One of the authors thus notes that he "is disturbed that he was not able to turn his critical eye on his own left-leaning, neo-Malthusian environmentalism of the time, which underlay much of his then tacit support for many aspects of the desertification narrative" (Moseley & Laris 2008, p. 73). Only in the years that followed in graduate school did he realize that it was highly problematic. Such metanarratives, in other words, can be both disarmingly simple and disarmingly effective at bridging the worlds of scientists, development practitioners and local populations. The distinction between basic social science, natural science and applied science furthermore is not useful here because it distracts from the ways the discourses in these spheres are entangled with each other. It is perhaps in part this bridging effect that gives such narratives their power through their interdisciplinary melding.

While doing research on flooding in northern Ghana, I thus found that ameliorating flooding was difficult not simply for technical reasons, but because dominant understandings of these semi-arid regions is locked into a desertification narrative that makes it difficult to change the interpretive framework on the terrain of facts alone. On the ground, the facts very clearly pointed to a problem of flooding, yet interlocutors kept returning to the problem of desertification.

Blaming the Local Victim to Make Room for the External Hero

> *I have heard about climate change. I have heard it on the radio [FM Bolga station], the radio tells us we should stop causing deforestation and stop burning the bush. If we stop, it will help us get better rains. If we don't and we continue, then we will get worse rains. If we deplete the forest and continue burning, it will rain where the forest is and leave the place that is bare with no or just light rain.*
> (Farmer, author interview, northern Ghana, March 2010)

In 2007, when the Bagré hydro-electric dam in Burkina Faso upstream from Ghana on the Volta River risked overflowing due to sudden heavy rains, water was released from the dam. This caused wide-ranging devastation downstream in northern Ghana, which was simultaneously also hit by the heavy rains: overflowing rivers, unbearably high humidity and large quantities of moving water as well as water accumulating in aberrant areas. During fieldwork, when I asked questions related to the flooding, informants would show me buildings and items ruined by the water (see Figure 5). Yet, even though they were showing me destruction from the flooding, we would often end up talking about drought. This became apparent, for example, when informants kept emphasizing the importance of planting trees because they would bring more rain. The conversation had inconspicuously changed from being about floods to being about the problem of drought, and, importantly, the problem of local resource mismanagement.

The importance attributed to trees was often linked to the desertification narrative, and the local population repeatedly explained that the planting of trees would lead to rainfall, while the cutting of trees would result in drought. They were thereby unknowingly echoing the aforementioned Charney hypothesis. The bias toward droughts also became clear when in 2010 I attended a seminar in Denmark entitled "Climate change – now what?," organized by a Danish NGO. The seminar included several participants from Ghana. Even though the images illustrating the seminar program depicted both drought and flooding, many of the speakers only talked about issues related to drought. For example, an official from the Environmental Protection Agency, Northern Region (Ghana) asserted: "Bush fires and the cutting of trees are the main problems." The seminar also featured four Ghanaian teachers doing a teacher exchange program in Denmark, who, as the program stated, would

A Bit Too Simple

Figure 5 Goats have moved into the ruins of a house destroyed by flooding. Ghana, March 2010. Photo by author.

"demonstrate, through a dramatic skit, the consequences of climate change for a family in northern Ghana." The skit turned out to be about tree cutting and bush fires. When a professor in agroecology, who was a member of the IPCC, gave a presentation that only discussed adaptation to drought, I asked why he did not talk about adaptation to flooding. He answered: "Adaptation strategies to flooding? That's correct, I haven't mentioned any. That's because they are more complicated." Flood control is in general a notoriously contested and complicated issue at social, economic and political levels, and therefore costly and difficult to implement (Colten 2009). Adaptation strategies to drought that are linked to changing local practices, on the other hand, provide an easier entry point for external interventions.

By pointing to the actions of "the victims" as problematic, interventions concerning desertification and drought focus primarily on the need to teach the local population better ways. They thereby underscore the importance of external intervention and make space for the NGOs to enter the story as heroes who save the local populations. Yet, flooding remains unaddressed and the local population is repeatedly treated as if their knowledge and practices are not just inappropriate but even villainous (Leach & Mearns 1996; Machaqueiro 2022). As I will discuss further in the following, this can lead to a debilitating sense of helplessness and even unwarranted feelings of ignorance and shame.

Internalizing Helplessness

Mette: Why do you think the flood happened?

Raymond: I don't know. I don't know what brought about that, so that is why I am afraid. Because if you know what brought about something, you may tackle it.

Mette: Did your teachers talk about the flooding when you returned to school?

Raymond: I never heard something about it from them ... It was something strange, I expected them to say something about it.

Mette: Do you have an idea why they didn't? [long pause] Why do you think they didn't [now addressing Lawrence]?

Lawrence: Well, one of the things is that our teachers, some of them didn't experience destruction from the flood, sometimes they didn't think of what happened. It may tend to be a laughing matter to them.

Mette: A laughing matter?

Lawrence: Yeah. Because, you see, they may group and say: "ah, water picked people away," [Raymond laughs] they are laughing like that. You see, you see that? Because, some of them, they are able to build houses out of cement [as opposed to just mud, which is more affordable] and the cement structures remain standing during flooding. Even some laugh, some people, because of that. They say, "Ay, you are just poor, living in a mud compound." You see? You know, the teachers think that a poor person has a poor mind.

(Author interview, northern Ghana, March 2010.
Raymond and Lawrence are pseudonyms)

As part of my fieldwork in the Upper East Region, I carried out interviews with young Ghanaians, some of whom, like Raymond, were still in high school. My local research assistant, Lawrence, was a recent high school graduate. The comment that some people think the poor deserve disasters because of their "poor mind," which angered Lawrence, can be linked to an internalization of inferiority that, in relation to colonialism, has been identified by the psychiatrist and political philosopher Frantz Fanon as a transformation of subjectivity that colonizes the mind (Fanon 1967). This form of oppression took place during colonial times through a "representation of the colonized in general as a people who are uncivilized, immoral, and devoid of values" (Sen 2020a, p. 66). Development narratives that represent the local population as unwitting villains and helpless victims in relation to climate change can have similar repercussions (Sultana 2022). Such narratives furthermore increasingly have the effect that "people in those countries are beginning to imagine the possible lives that might be available 'out there' because they are often convinced that life is 'better' elsewhere" (Salazar 2011, p. 578), and this can lead to out-migration.

In the Upper East Region, development narratives can have a strong impact on the local population and their imaginaries because of the development sector's prominence in the area (Olwig 2012, 2013; Olwig & Gough 2013). In places like the Upper East Region, development intervention, according to development scholar Christian Lund, "is so significant a practice in the form of development aid, and macro-economic and political conditionality, that it must constitute a primary object of empirical research and theoretical concern" (Lund 2010, p. 22). Northern Ghana is markedly poorer than southern Ghana, and this is often attributed to its lower agroecological potential compared with the wetter south. Colonial and postcolonial development strategies furthermore favored the south, which, in addition to higher agroecological potential, included opportunities for large-scale gold mining and cocoa farming. This has led to labor outmigration and poor infrastructure in the north (Songsore 2011; Whitehead 2006). At the time of my research, there was little by way of industry or bigger businesses in the region, and the development sector was therefore not only a potential source of resources and support, it was also a sector that offered one of few, relatively well-paid career pathways for those who were able to afford a university education. In several villages, there were multiple NGOs, many of which were local but funded by large international development donors. Through my research, I observed how the language, narratives and rationalities associated with development traveled from donor institutions such as the World Bank in Washington, DC, through NGO offices and to local communities in Bolgatanga. As a result, I would hear remarkably similar statements whether sitting with community members who had been summoned by an NGO for a meeting under a baobab tree in Bolgatanga or interviewing officials working in a World Bank office in Washington, DC (Olwig 2012, 2013). The development sector and its rationalities and narratives represent a huge force in northern Ghana, and it is therefore in a powerful position to also influence the minds of the local people.

Not knowing or understanding a phenomenon such as flooding shapes local imaginaries, fears, hopes and strategies. Combining this with the systematic devaluing of local knowledge and the villainizing of local practices that accompany development hero metanarratives on the environment and increasingly climate change, it is understandable that the external view of local people as helpless and in need of external expertise could be internalized (Olwig 2012, 2013; Sultana 2022). Yet, as my conversation with Raymond and Lawrence indicates, there is also resistance – Raymond expected more from the teacher and Lawrence was angry. There is a growing academic literature emphasizing the importance of acknowledging resistance, especially in relation to climate mitigation and adaptation projects. This research focuses on "the agency of the individuals, families and communities that leverage, and at other times resist or rework, an adaptation project through quotidian struggles and engagements in and with these initiatives" (Mills-Novoa et al. 2023, p. 2287). Such resistance exists not only locally (Nielsen 2010; Sørensen 2008) but also through international movements. Thus, in recent years, Indigenous and environmental movements as well as transnational alliances and coalitions such as the Alliance of Small Island States are increasingly challenging what geographer Farhana Sultana refers to as "climate coloniality" (2022). Lawrence and the other people I talked with in the Upper East Region therefore might be even angrier today and aware of the issue of climate injustice.

This section has presented three key stereotypical characters that often drive forward the simplifying crisis storyline in development hero metanarratives, and shown how they may induce local people to feel inadequate, helpless and in need of "heroic" intervention to be "saved." It has further discussed the negative repercussions of certain narratives becoming dominant, cutting across sectors, and generally shaping mental images of an area. This was exemplified by how the desertification narrative hampered the development of potentially constructive solutions to other environmental problems, such as uncontrolled floods. However, the section has also presented evidence that local people can be critical of, and angered by, development hero metanarratives that blame them for local disasters and result in inadequate policies and interventions. This leads to counter stories and accounts, like that of Raymond and Lawrence, which need to be taken seriously if development initiatives are to succeed.

Section 4 will go into more detail on how the characters of the victim, villain and hero, and their role in development hero metanarratives, affect the way solutions are imagined and implemented. But it will also show how such narratives become challenged when attention is directed toward locally grounded stories and the knowledge and experiences they represent.

4 Solutions: How Trees Became the Answer to Climate Change

Uncritical approaches to carbon offsets and credits are good examples of how dominant metanarratives can lead to oversimplified solutions to complex challenges. Buying carbon credits that represent carbon sequestration through (CO_2 absorbing) forestry is a commonly proposed solution to climate change. This solution can be compared to buying indulgences that bring absolution for the human sin of increasing CO_2 levels. This line of thought thereby resembles the declensionist plot, discussed in Section 3, and its focus on human sin leading to the loss of an ideal Edenic natural state. In addition to buying carbon credits, individual tree planting is also encouraged. Indeed, carbon sequestration through forestry as a solution to climate change is widely promoted via campaigns and initiatives by civil society, the private sector, and intergovernmental and governmental organizations, often captured by the simple slogan "plant a tree." It is exactly due to the apparent simplicity of the solution that it is easily promoted – all you need is a seedling and some soil – and anyone can therefore seemingly help by planting (or paying to have planted) a tree anywhere. Yet, when the solution becomes too simple, many nuances are lost. Tree planting as a climate change solution risks reducing climate change to being simply a matter of carbon emissions, yet successful tree planting and climate change mitigation involve more than carbon sequestration (Fischer et al. 2019). Furthermore, many of these initiatives do not lead to trees being planted by just "anyone" or "anywhere." Many are planted in the Global South under the aegis of external actors, including for-profits as well as non-profits (Fischer et al. 2019; Machaqueiro 2022; Svarstad & Benjaminsen 2017). This is problematically justified in part by articulating local behavior in relation to forests as inappropriate ("villainous"), thereby leading to the need for external actors ("heroes") to "civilize" local forest management. We thus see influential climate change narratives converging with the familiar development hero metanarrative discussed in Section 3.

In 2013, I was part of a small pilot research project studying land acquisitions by external investors who established tree plantations in Tanzania for paper production, lumber, poles, furniture and carbon credits. Between 2016 and 2022, I participated in a larger research project in southern Ghana investigating the biophysical and socioeconomic aspects of agroforestry as climate change adaptation in the cocoa sector. This project explored the sustainability of cocoa agroforestry – "the growing of cocoa together with shade trees and food crops for agronomic, economic and environmental benefits" (Olwig et al. 2024a, p. 3). In this section, drawing on these projects, I will illuminate how trees can be highly beneficial, but that solutions that promote undifferentiated and monocrop tree planting are problematic – for people, the environment and the planet. Such solutions arguably support the geopolitical status quo rather than ecosystems and populations, particularly in the Global South.

Heroic Solutions or Climate Coloniality?

REDD+ aims to incentivize developing countries to contribute to climate change mitigation actions in the forest sector by:

- *reducing carbon emissions from deforestation;*
- *reducing carbon emissions from forest degradation;*
- *conservation of forest carbon stocks;*

- *sustainable management of forests; and*
- *enhancement of forest carbon stocks.*

(UN-REDD Programme 2016, p. 1)

REDD+ constitutes a climate change mitigation solution developed by Parties to the UNFCCC, and is a concrete and prominent example of an initiative that has a strong focus on tree planting and carbon credits. In the UN description of REDD+ quoted here, "sustainable management of forests" gets only one bullet point, the other four points being singularly focused on carbon, thus illustrating the tendency to be concerned primarily with an excess of CO_2. Moreover, REDD+ is only addressing so-called *developing countries*, presenting them as needing to be *incentivized*. It is once again the local population in the Global South that is problematically framed as mismanaging the environment.

As discussed in the previous sections, beginning under colonialism, populations in the Global South have been blamed for destroying the forest. This critique has been directed in particular toward shifting cultivation, which can be described as "a land use strategy often applied by resource-poor households, [that] is based on the rotation of fields rather than crops and relies on the use of fallowing to sustain production of food crops" (Bruun et al. 2021, p. 1). There are many types of fallow systems, yet researchers and policymakers problematically tend to group them together (Boserup 1965).

Research is still only beginning to comprehend the carbon outcomes of transitioning from shifting cultivation to other land uses, in part due to the fact that carbon is not just stored above ground, but also below ground in the root biomass and the soil. Findings indicate that in some instances, shifting cultivation leads to higher carbon storage as well as better outcomes in relation to several other socioeconomic and environmental benefits compared to other land use types (Bruun et al. 2021; Martin et al. 2023; Ziegler et al. 2012). Shifting cultivation has also been argued to be not only "a necessary risk aversion strategy perfectly adapted to local ecological circumstances, but also a strategy that allowed farmers to maintain possession over their means of production" (Machaqueiro 2022, p. 212). Nevertheless, as with the desertification narrative discussed in Section 3, dominant, oversimplified and misleading assumptions concerning shifting cultivation have led to widespread perceptions that shifting cultivation causes degradation and a reduction in carbon storage.

In many countries, REDD+ projects have ended up focusing on eliminating shifting cultivation and establishing fortress conservation and afforestation initiatives. This reflects the questionable, yet familiar storyline of external actors (the heroes) needing to teach (incentivize) the local people in the Global South (the villains) about the importance of changing their behavior to bring them salvation, and how to do so. As noted, such initiatives have been referred to as "climate coloniality." Sultana writes: "Simultaneously, the colonial white gaze that saw non-white Others as inferior and lacking continues to desire to 'fix' the 'third world' and further white saviorism in climate solutions" (Sultana 2022, p. 6).

The climate solution that involves actors in the Global North paying to have trees safeguarded and/or planted in the Global South fits a hero narrative well. Following this narrative storyline, the solution is "salvational" in all three senses of the word: "deliverance from the power and effects of sin" (the sin of emitting CO_2), "liberation from ignorance or illusion" (incentivizing the local population to change what is believed to be ignorant behavior), and "preservation from destruction or failure" (saving the local people from the negative repercussions of their own villainous behavior) (Merriam-Webster 2023). The result of this type of solution is often that people in the Global South are expected to change their behavior, potentially affecting their ability to make a livelihood, while the people in the Global North are relatively unaffected.

Several studies show that using afforestation to reduce atmospheric CO_2 is "land hungry" (Bond et al. 2019, p. 964). There is a limit to how much land can be used for this purpose and, as a result, such initiatives have a limited effect, serving rather as a distraction "from the serious business of reducing emissions by reducing fossil fuel use" (Bond et al. 2019, p. 963). This fossil fuel use reduction must take place in the Global North in order to adequately mitigate climate change. Yet, it is in the interest of several different groups of stakeholders to articulate carbon credits generated through tree planting in the Global South and purchased by actors in the Global North, as a preferred climate change solution. It makes consumers and CO_2 emitters in the Global North feel good, or better, about their emissions, because they have both paid for their sins and supposedly helped a suffering population. As Mutua points out in the context of human rights, this type of salvational solution can also be linked to "the redemption of the redeemers, in which whites who are privileged globally as a people – who have historically visited untold suffering and savage atrocities against non-whites – redeem themselves by 'defending' and 'civilizing' 'lower,' 'unfortunate,' and 'inferior' peoples" (Mutua 2001, pp. 207–208; see also Richey & Ponte 2011).

Carbon credits are in the interest of policymakers in the Global North because carbon credits enable them to avoid having to implement potentially unpopular policies in the Global North such as reducing consumption and production-based emissions. Additionally, carbon credits can legitimize external afforestation interventions in the name of carbon sequestration – even if these interventions negatively affect local populations. REDD+ is categorized as a "natural" solution to climate change, and since nature "is often seen as being intrinsically good, ideal, and in need of human protection," this can be a "powerful political tool" (Osaka et al. 2021, p. 12). The idea of natural solutions to climate change, sometimes referred to as ecosystem-based solutions, nature-based solutions or natural climate solutions, has gained traction in part as a result of a romanticization of nature in line with the declensionist narrative and are supported by many conservation NGOs, finance institutions, think tanks, businesses and development aid agencies (Asiyanbi & Lund 2020; Machaqueiro 2022). But framing solutions such as tree planting as natural can have the effect that attention is "diverted from the actual qualities of a policy and replaced with a general sense of the 'goodness' or 'rightness' of such interventions" (Osaka et al. 2021, p. 13). Indeed, several of these so-called natural solutions to climate change have been contested by Indigenous Peoples and local communities that have described them as "carbon colonialism" (Townsend et al. 2020, p. 553). When "natural" solutions such as afforestation do not account for the complexity of the local socioeconomic and ecological context, they have been shown to negatively impact livelihoods, biodiversity and food security – even their impact on carbon storage can be unclear (Bond et al. 2019; Osaka et al. 2021).

Monocrop Commercial Forest Plantations as Good Solutions to Climate Change?

When climate change becomes simplified as entirely a problem of excess CO_2 in the atmosphere, this can lead to trees becoming simplified to be primarily carbon-absorbers. Trees are thereby effectively reduced to units of countable carbon, and are turned into abstract, quantifiable entities. Structural issues and power dynamics are effectively downplayed and tree planting is conveniently (and incorrectly) presented as an apolitical and technical solution (cf. Ferguson 1994; Fischer & Hajdu 2018; Li 2007). It does not matter what tree is being planted, by whom or where. As a result, any action perceived to destroy trees, such as shifting cultivation, is presented as bad, and any form of tree planting, regardless of the biophysical and socioeconomic impacts of the trees, is presented as good. This makes it possible to frame monocrop commercial forest plantations as good solutions to climate change. In this blog story posted by *Paper Advance: News for the Paper Industry Professional*, for-profit plantations that continuously plant, fell and replant fast-growing trees are for example presented as an excellent form of carbon storage:

> Creating tree plantations for the purpose of using their wood supply is a positive step in terms of carbon stocks, since establishment of plantations stores carbon permanently, which planting annual crops does not do. In

addition, some of the wood from plantations may go into solid wood products with a long lifetime, resulting in further carbon storage. (Fairbank 2019)

The private Norwegian company Green Resources provides a good example of a for-profit endeavor that is presented as a good solution to climate change. During the time of our research in Tanzania, Green Resources was a significant actor in relation to forestry, being the largest forest development and wood processing company in East Africa managing plantation forests in Mozambique, Tanzania and Uganda. On their website, Green Resources has stated that it "is actively combatting climate change by planting new forests."[5]

The plantation company, as well as many other tree planting initiatives, have further emphasized that in addition to combatting climate change, the plantations can improve the socioeconomic condition of the local populations. As Green Resources stated on its website: "We believe that forestation is one of the most efficient ways of improving social and economic conditions for people in rural areas."[6] Indeed, the Norwegian Agency for Development Cooperation (NORAD) has presented Green Resources as a strategic partner and Green Resources has benefitted from NORAD funding in several ways.[7,8] Furthermore, Green Resources has acquired both Forest Stewardship Council (FSC) certification for several of its plantations and it has also been engaged in Voluntary Carbon Standard (VCS) certification.[9,10] International afforestation is an important part of the climate change mitigation policy of Norway, an oil-producing country: "it is seen [to be] more cost-effective to mitigate climate change in a low-cost country, rather than in an expensive country like Norway" (Svarstad & Benjaminsen 2017, p. 483). Yet, as we found in the research project on land acquisitions in Tanzania, these forests are often profit-oriented plantations consisting almost exclusively of only two types of trees, fast-growing Eucalyptus and Pinus trees, and they benefit primarily the shareholders at the expense of both the local people and the environment (Olwig et al. 2015).

As will be further elaborated, the dominant solution of tree planting takes focus away from the fact that undifferentiated tree planting can harm the environment and have a negative impact on people's socioeconomic conditions. Indeed, undifferentiated tree planting, especially in the form of monocrop forest plantations, can lead to a reduction in biodiversity (see Figure 6), and can even

---

[5] https://greenresources.no (accessed July 11, 2025).
[6] Ibid.
[7] Overview of projects funded by NORAD involving Green Resources as a partner can be found here: https://resultater.norad.no/prosjekter-resultater (accessed July 14, 2025).
[8] Refseth, T. H. D. (2010). *Norwegian Carbon Plantations in Tanzania: Towards Sustainable Development?* Masters' thesis, Norwegian University of Life Sciences.
[9] Ibid.
[10] https://greenresources.no/about/ (accessed July 11, 2025).

Figure 6 Forest plantations often exhibit low biodiversity. This photograph shows a section of Green Resources Mapanda Forest Plantation, Tanzania, June 2013. Photo by Christine Noe.

result in a decrease in carbon storage as it may disturb existing ecosystems that are better at absorbing carbon. This is in part because in many ecosystems, as noted, most carbon is stored in the soil, and research has shown that, for example, heathland, moorland and grassland can have higher soil carbon storage than forest plantations (Bond et al. 2019; Friggens et al. 2020). Important questions arising in relation to tree planting as a solution thus include: Which species of tree is being planted? Where will this tree be planted? What do the trees replace? Who will take care of the trees? What resources are diverted to care for the trees and what would they have been used for otherwise? Who benefits from the trees? The next subsection delves into these questions.

(All) Trees are Good? For Whom and For What?

There were several shade trees, and he showed us an avocado tree and a tree that [the extension officer] had explained could provide oil from its fruits that he could sell – but [the extension officer] had yet to show him how. There were also orange trees and pawpaw. They only used oranges for domestic consumption because it is difficult to make money from them – when in season they sell for very little as opposed to cocoa, which has the same government-set price throughout the season. Orange trees are also not very functional as shade trees. In addition, there were banana plants, which provide important shade for the cocoa seedlings and produce fruits for domestic consumption. Some are also sold on the market. Otherwise, the shade trees on his cocoa farm were mostly useful as timber. At one point he shows us a mahogany tree that he is expecting to make a lot of money from when he cuts it. He had planted more than one when [the extension officer's] project was going on, but only one had survived and even though he had tried to prune it, it had not grown very tall before sprouting branches.

(Field notes, cocoa farm visit, southern Ghana, November 2018)

A tree is a tree is a tree? Trees absorb carbon, but the many other attributes of trees vary immensely. During fieldwork on cocoa farms in Ghana in 2018, our research team toured farmers' fields to gain a better understanding of the opportunities and challenges of agroforestry. Agroforestry is linked to climate change both because integrating shade trees into cocoa farming is able to mitigate some of the negative impacts of climate change such as heat and drought, and because shade trees sequester carbon (Olwig et al. 2024c).

While showing us around on their cocoa farms, the farmers explained why they had, or had not, planted non-cocoa trees on their farms. They also discussed which types of trees they had planted, and why. In total, the team found 111 different tree species on the cocoa plots.[11] The reasoning for planting these trees included the varying needs for shade, food and timber (see Figure 7). For example, different levels of shade were essential at different stages in the growth of the cocoa tree, and different levels of shade and combinations of

Figure 7 Cocoa-agroforestry systems are comprised of cocoa trees (center), planted alongside other species of trees such as timber-producing trees such as mahogany (left), and fruit trees such as orange trees (right), as well as food crops like plantain and cassava (left). Ghana, November 2018.
Photos by author.

---

[11] Boadi, S. A. (2021). *Socio-economic Potential of Agroforestry as an Alternative Livelihood Strategy for Cocoa Farmers in Ghana*. Doctoral dissertation, University of Ghana.

shade tree species could result in different levels and types of pests and diseases and cocoa yields (Olwig et al. 2024b). Similarly, edible tree crops were valuable at different times and in different ways. Some fruits were useful for eating on the spot while working on the cocoa farm, some could be sold and some were important for household food security. Regarding timber, some timber trees were valuable for sale, while others grew fast and could be of immediate use to the household. Timber trees posed a particular challenge for farmers, as the farmers were not allowed to cut the trees, and in effect did not have the rights to a tree, unless they could prove that they had planted or nurtured it, which would then allow them to obtain a permit from the Forestry Commission of Ghana. Yet, obtaining this permit was bureaucratically complicated and often involved fees (Bosselman et al. 2024).

Another important concern for the cocoa farmer was that some types of trees are more labor-intensive than others. As one farmer explained to us, "some trees require a lot of attention especially those in bad soils or whose roots require a lot of moisture, and some need a lot of time, even compared to cocoa" (field notes, southern Ghana, November 2018). Cocoa farmers also described how they had to remove trees because they created problems: "She had some shade trees in one plot, and none in the other. She chose to leave many of the trees to die by cutting the bark away in a circle around the tree because the trees took too many nutrients" (field notes, southern Ghana, November 2018). Other shade trees can positively impact nutrients and soil characteristics. Furthermore, different shade tree species impact the broader complex of plant species involved differently. Cocoa agroforestry does not just include trees, but also other types of plants, such as plantain, cocoyam and cassava, that each interact in specific ways with various tree species influencing their productivity.

Whether the farmers saw any benefits to planting a tree on their farm depended in part on the many different attributes of the tree in question. Yet, only recently has research and policy on cocoa agroforestry begun to distinguish between different shade tree species and investigate the impacts of different levels of diversity in relation to shade tree species (Boadi et al. 2024). It is important to consider shade tree diversity in relation to both biophysical factors (e.g., rates of pests and diseases and competition between trees for nutrients and water) and socioeconomic factors (e.g., costs and benefits, food security, labor needs). However, many extension services, whether provided by the state, the cocoa industry or NGOs, only offer a minimal selection of shade tree seedlings when working with farmers to implement cocoa agroforestry (Olwig et al. 2024b). Agroforestry as climate change adaptation will only succeed if local knowledge of tree species based on lived experience is listened to, included and prioritized.

The consequences on the ground of not distinguishing between different tree species were also apparent in the study of tree plantations in Tanzania. The problem of reducing trees to a means of carbon sequestration was particularly pronounced. The study area at the time of research had experienced a dramatic rise in conservation and commercial forestry projects, and therefore had the most extensive forest cover in the region. The Tanzanian subsidiary of the Norwegian Green Resources was one of the biggest investors in the area and had secured ninety-nine–year leases on more than a quarter of the total area of the two villages included in our study. Between 2001 and 2012, the annual number of trees planted rose from around 3.5 million to more than 31 million, and the area was identified in 2008 by the Tanzanian Vice President's office as a National Carbon Credit pilot area (Olwig et al. 2015, p. 2329).

While an increase in forest cover enhances forest carbon stocks in line with the aims of REDD+, some tree species, such as the various subspecies of Pinus and Eucalyptus that make up the majority of Green Resources plantations, can cause local environmental problems, including nutrient depletion and water deficiency. Eucalyptus especially has an extremely high water-demand and flammability, increasing the risk of high-severity fires (Bond et al. 2019; Machaqueiro 2022; Purdon 2013). More than a fifth of the residents surveyed in the study area as part of the research project in fact identified water scarcity as their main environmental concern. Almost half also mentioned that in the past ten years they had experienced a decrease in water resources (Olwig et al. 2015).

A Forest Is Better Than Other Nature?

We have so far seen several examples of trees being simplistically favored compared to other types of vegetation, with problematic consequences. Another consequence is that rural land that is neither forested nor intensively cultivated becomes considered idle or waste land of no value (Gausset & Whyte 2012; Noe 2013; Olwig et al. 2015; Shivji 2009). Furthermore:

> global maps of "deforestation" and "degradation" ... erroneously assume that low tree cover, in climates that can support forests, are "deforested" and "degraded." The bizarre result is that ancient savanna landscapes, including the Serengeti and Kruger National Park, are mapped as deforested and degraded (because tree cover is reduced by elephants, antelope, and several million years of grass-fuelled fires). (Bond et al. 2019, p. 963)

Since the colonial era, the inability to acknowledge the value of other types of land use, such as commons used for extensive grazing or land set aside for shifting cultivation, has led to land being considered underutilized and therefore as being available for enclosure (Gausset & Whyte 2012). In Europe in the eighteenth century, commons were similarly enclosed and often afforested according to the logic that land that was not owned and managed by a private owner, but rather by a collectivity sharing its resources, was underutilized. Enclosure was thus thought to be beneficial both economically and environmentally (Gausset & Whyte 2012; Olwig et al. 2015). By turning the common land into enclosed forest land, private landowners, industry and the state were able to benefit from it, but this came at the expense of the people who depended on the commons for their livelihood.

In Tanzania, we found that many of the tree plantations were being established on village land that had not previously been forested. This was justified by investors and local governments by depicting the land as idle or underutilized. However, this land can be very important environmentally, economically and socially. Economically and socially, we found that the land had traditionally been used seasonally for field rotation and as family reserves that comprised ancestral graveyards and ritual sites. It was also an economic resource that could be inherited by future generations or gifted to a friend or relative in need (Olwig et al. 2015, p. 2323). From an environmental perspective, grass- and scrublands that are being afforested through large-scale monocrop forest plantations often result in biodiversity reduction. Furthermore, as noted, forest plantations can lead to water loss in the surrounding ecosystem (Silveira & Alonso 2009).

It is also problematic when monocrop forest plantations replace local trees, which grow both in forests and on grass- and scrublands. Studies have shown how local populations actively use a diversity of local trees (Fischer et al. 2019), and how forests contribute to livelihoods and food security through "subsistence use of products, such as food, fodder, and medicinal plants; cash income obtained from sale of products; and more indirect ecological benefits such as the contributions of forests and trees to agricultural productivity" (Rasmussen et al. 2017, p. 1). A study of a Green Resources plantation in Uganda found that the establishment of monocrop tree plantations not only "reduced the diversity of trees available in that area, replacing them with two foreign species," it also forced the local population to "use the land outside the plantation more intensively, contributing to a further reduction in trees in those areas" (Fischer et al. 2019, p. 192).

As mentioned earlier, commercial forest plantations have been supported by aid agencies such as NORAD, using the rationale that they can save both the planet and support the local population. Local people, the argument goes, can potentially benefit from employment on the plantations, from partaking in the carbon economy and from the "community development" or "social services" such as energy-saving stoves, schools or other infrastructure that the investors promise to provide in exchange for being allowed to lease the land (Fischer et al. 2019; Purdon 2013). At the time of our study in Tanzania, however, only a small percentage of the local people engaged in timber trading and lumbering (2 and

2.7 percent, respectively), and a mere 6.7 percent worked on the plantations as casual laborers (Olwig et al. 2015, p. 2327). Furthermore, our research as well as several other studies have documented local frustration with the expected social services and promised community development initiatives because they are often excessively delayed or in other ways do not live up to the promises made (Fischer et al. 2019; Purdon 2013). Commitment to deliver such social services is nevertheless an important part of the process that enables the investors to acquire land, but which in effect constitutes only a symbolic compensation (Locher & Sulle 2013). The money paid for leasing the land is often much lower than the market price, and in some cases, no compensation is given at all. A study of land acquisitions in Tanzania from 2009, for example, found that "compensation stood at approximately 6–13% of the value of total lands acquired" (Purdon 2013, p. 1143). Finally, studies have shown that obtaining the certification needed for the local population to benefit from the carbon economy involves so much bureaucracy and technocratic knowledge that communities risk becoming dependent on external assistance (Mwamfupe et al. 2022). There is thus little indication that the commercial forest plantations live up to their promises in relation to either the environmental or the socioeconomic aspects.

This section has shown how simplifying metanarratives can lead to oversimplified solutions, such as carbon offsetting, that have problematic consequences. The solution of carbon offsetting makes it possible for countries in the Global North, which are historically responsible for climate change, to continue emitting carbon while promoting high mass consumption as long as they pay (through carbon credits) for the absolution of their carbon sins. But this leads to undifferentiated tree planting, including establishing for-profit monocrop forest plantations, which ironically often takes place in the Global South and has questionable socio-environmental outcomes. Nevertheless, such tree planting is justified through narratives that build on the familiar development hero metanarrative about bringing salvation to the local population who have supposedly mismanaged their natural resources. Undifferentiated tree planting as the salvational solution to climate change is not just convenient in its simplicity, it is also a means of maintaining the status quo.

So far in this Element, profit-making has lurked in the shadows of strategic partnerships with industry and companies in initiatives that claim to simultaneously save the planet and the people. However, in recent years, there has been a change whereby "profit-making" and "making a difference" in relation to development, sustainability and climate change are presented as not only compatible, but mutually co-dependent. This is the topic of Section 5.

5 For-Profit Characters and Storylines: Sustainability Superheroes and Profitable Redemption

"How do you know the stories you are telling are for a good idea? What makes something a good idea?" Our answer at the time was, "well if you're asking that question ... [members of the audience giggle] it is probably not a good idea that you are working on [general laughter]!" And then we thought, it's a bit of a copout, there's gotta be a better answer to that. And we were founded in 2015 ... well it is a bit of a no-brainer, there's a pretty good list of what makes something a good idea. So that's now what we do as a business, we work on ideas that essentially further one of these goals ... [I look up just long enough to see the SDGs flash across the screen before the speaker moves on].

(Field notes, Denmark, October 2017)

The consultant cited here was presenting at a workshop held by a British communications agency that focused on how business best promote their "good ideas." The consultants were using the term "good" in two ways, with one meaning being a sound idea and the other being an idea that is identifiable with "doing good." As he indicated in the quote, many businesses found that with the introduction of the SDGs, they were provided with a convenient and visible narrative framework for explaining and marketing development, sustainability and climate change efforts. "Doing good" is a vague concept. It has been defined rather broadly in the business literature as, for example, "to serve some larger social purpose besides making profits" (Karnani 2011) or to "make the world a better place" (Falck & Heblich 2007). As part of its promotion of the SDGs, the UN created websites that included definitions, descriptions and targets for each goal. Thus, with the new SDG framework, a business could now justify that they were "doing good," simply by referring to a particular goal and the arguments put forward by the UN (Engberg-Pedersen & Fejerskov 2018).

This section will discuss how for-profit hero metanarratives of doing good gained prominence as for-profits were given an increasingly central role in addressing sustainability, climate change and development through the SDGs. It examines the ways in which these for-profit hero metanarratives convey and shape incentives, rationalities and ideologies in relation to how solutions to challenges concerning development, sustainability and climate change are imagined, practiced and legitimated. In particular, it argues that these for-profit hero metanarratives promote the disputed belief that "profit-making" and "making a difference" are mutually dependent.

This section is based on field methods including participant observation, text analysis and online ethnographic research. Fieldwork was undertaken at conferences and seminars between 2017 and 2019 on topics of relevance to combining profit-making with doing good. This type of ethnography is called "event ethnography" (Campbell et al. 2014; Christiansen & Olwig 2019; MacDonald 2010; Olwig & Christiansen 2015; Postill 2024). The study focused on the narratives emerging from presentations and conversations at conferences and workshops targeting businesses concerned with sustainability, climate change and development. The businesses were international and national, but the fieldwork took place in Denmark, a frontrunner SDG country (Sachs et al. 2019).

Development Frameworks: The SDGs

Development frameworks, such as the SDGs, tell an overarching story that structures the work of the overall development sector in relation to which NGOs and other relevant actors must position themselves. The introduction of a new official UN-sanctioned development framework, and the narratives it represents, configures and further promotes, thus has important repercussions (Fukuda-Parr 2016; Fukuda-Parr & McNeill 2019). With the SDGs, the UN broadened their development framework to include challenges outside the Global South, such as environmental problems in the Global North. One key aspect of the SDGs was thus that they were defined as pertaining to *global* social, economic and environmental challenges, and thereby relevant for everyone and everywhere – indeed, they are also known as the Global Goals. Framing the SDGs as relevant globally appeared to redress the problem of development being perceived and presented as the "superior" *West* saving the "needy" *Rest*. This framework thereby responded to a widespread popular aversion to the development sector that in part was spurred by academic critique of development as promoting Western hegemony and ideology leading to a post-development school that gained ground in the 1990s (e.g., Escobar 1995).

The SDG framework was further lauded for addressing some of the critique of earlier state-centered development frameworks, such as the MDGs. The MDGs were seen to contribute to a North–South hierarchical binary because they were presented as only relevant for countries in the Global South. Furthermore, they were critiqued for ignoring that processes of development involve hybrid transnational actors and alliances crossing national boundaries, and that inequality within countries is growing worldwide (Horner & Hulme 2019; Richey 2014). Indeed, in recent years, the type, variety and alliances of development actors have multiplied to include industrializing countries, post-socialist states and new global powers and development banks. Furthermore, several different actor categories, such as businesses, local elites, consumers, tourists, diaspora groups and philanthropists, have grown in importance (e.g., Budabin & Richey 2018; Kapoor 2013; Kragelund 2019; Mostafanezhad 2014; Richey & Ponte 2011).

The SDGs provided more opportunities for actors such as businesses to be involved in, and benefit from, the development sector. There is a long history of development institutions, on the one hand, supporting Global North businesses' entrance into Global South markets and, on the other hand, fostering business-to-business partnerships intended to encourage Global North businesses to build the capacity of Global South businesses (Brogaard & Petersen 2018). The SDGs were thus part of a longer process of engaging business in challenges at the intersection of the environment and development, which arguably began with the 1987 Brundtland Report on sustainable development (Scheyvens et al. 2016, p. 372). While the relationship between business and development is deep-rooted and complex, the SDGs directly promoted, rationalized, legitimized and institutionalized this relationship. Business furthermore played a key role in formulating the SDGs, thereby both ideologically and in practice shaping, while also being shaped by, development institutions (Mawdsley 2018; Scheyvens et al. 2016; van Zanten & van Tulder 2018).

An important reason given for why business attained a key role in relation to the SDGs was that the goals could not be reached using traditional measures of development financing, such as overseas development assistance (ODA) (Mawdsley 2018). With the importance of business investments as a funding mechanism for the SDGs, for-profits gained a greater role in determining what aspects of "sustainable development" would be addressed. My research showed that there was a tendency for businesses to focus on goals and targets that could maximize market opportunities while avoiding goals, such as SDG 10 on inequalities, that might raise questions about their practices and the overall systemic power relations from which they benefitted.

This selectivity, however, was not challenged at the events I attended. Indeed, two consultants presenting at the same event, who were part of two different projects helping business incorporate the SDGs, both independently emphasized that not all the goals are relevant for business. In fact, both consultants contended that only a third of the targets and indicators were applicable for business, the rest being for other actors to act on. The SDGs themselves, in other words, reflect certain implicit presumptions concerning the province of the public sector versus the private sector. One of the consultants had the following recommendation on his presentation slide entitled "Integrating SDGs for Business Impact": "Focus on specific SDGs and integrate with financial and business targets" (field notes, Denmark, May 2019). The other consultant, who worked for the UN, explained during his presentation that the types of SDG targets relevant for business could be divided into three categories: 1) Legislation and standards, which includes environmental standards, working conditions and rights; 2) Operational and supply chain practices, which include employee conditions and energy efficiency; and 3) Market opportunities and innovation, which include the need for access to safe drinking water, adequate food and medicine (field notes, Denmark, May 2019). This selectivity driven by for-profit logics impeded an integrated approach, where the synergies, trade-offs and links between goals are addressed and grounded in the needs of those affected.

The SDGs facilitated that businesses could actively market their overall enterprise as doing good. This marketing is similar to other business practices aimed at creating a positive brand such as corporate social responsibility (CSR) initiatives, "brand aid," cause-related marketing and the use of fair trade–certified and/or environmentally friendly ingredients and products (Hawkins 2012; Jamali & Keshishian 2009; Lekakis 2012; Richey & Ponte 2011). Yet, one major difference is that from the perspective of the businesses, these practices were previously often add-ons and done in collaboration with non-profits that used partnerships with businesses, or the sale of products, to fundraise. Many for-profits engaged in the SDGs, however, framed doing good as part of their core business, and not just as an add-on, while non-profits now increasingly fundraise and boost their brand through the sale of products, experiences and entertainment (Chouliaraki & Vestergaard 2022; Kapoor 2013; Richey & Ponte 2011; Vestergaard 2008). These developments indicate changes in the relation between doing good and making a profit.

Sustainability: The Right and Profitable Thing to Do

Sustainability! I like the word. To be sustainable – what is it then? ... It is the right thing to do, it is the smart thing to do, but the good thing now is that it has actually, it has become legal [legitimate] to say that it's the profitable thing to do. It is actually ok to talk about investing in companies that have an agenda which is sustainability or impact and then expect a return on investments. That's a new thing! It's a great thing! Because now we are opening up for the big bucks. [The Danish "angel investor"[12] adds that her company today has an impact agenda. While drawing a heart on the whiteboard behind her, she clarifies:] *When we five years ago talked about impact investing, we talked about doing it solely from the heart. As a private investor, you invest in an impact business because you like the cause ... And you do it, and you do it heart and soul ... but the great thing is, it's ok to talk about the cash.* [She draws "+$" next to the heart.] *And that development is fine, it's good.*

(Field notes, investor pitch, Denmark, December 2018)

---

[12] A person who, usually in return for equity, gives advice to, and infuses capital in, start-ups.

Different types of actors pushed businesses to engage with the SDGs. Government policies worldwide increasingly require companies to provide environmental and social protection and to conform to a growing number of international agreements on climate change, human rights and labor conditions. Furthermore, civil society organizations and social movements have responded to changing norms and values by placing greater emphasis on ethics and sustainability in production (Ponte 2019; van Zanten & van Tulder 2018). Businesses, however, are not only pressured by society and governments. They have themselves chosen to assume a more active role in promoting private-sector solutions. They do so by "positively shaping sustainability discourses and practices, first by becoming engaged in self-regulatory and market-based initiatives aimed at improving the environmental impact of their operations, and then by identifying ways in which value could be created and captured through sustainability management" (Ponte 2019, pp. 13–14). In effect, this becomes what we could call a form of profitable redemption.

One reason why the SDGs were attractive to businesses is that business had an influential role in developing the SDGs (Scheyvens et al. 2016, p. 371).[13] It was apparent at events I attended that the businesses felt they were being taken seriously as important partners in the promotion of sustainable development. Corporate presenters clearly expressed a sense of pride in having been called to action by former UN Secretary-General Bank Ki-Moon and an appreciation for the business sector being included from the beginning of the negotiations. While the SDGs in general were considered to have consulted many relevant actors, the previous UN goals, the MDGs, were criticized for excluding several actors, including businesses. As one presenter exclaimed: "MDGs were a closed club for certain people, certain government officials. The private sector was not invited in!" (field notes, Denmark, March 2018).

Another reason why businesses embraced the SDGs is that with their colorful and recognizable logos they offered a useful branding tool that could increase business opportunities. The ability of businesses to make a profit, of course, is one of the reasons they are highlighted as powerful partners (cf. Prudham 2009). This accords with SDG 17, which encourages partnerships between governments, the private sector and civil society, urging that action is "needed to mobilize, redirect and unlock the transformative power of trillions of dollars of private resources to deliver on sustainable development objectives" (United Nations n.d.). Like the angel investor cited earlier, a UN consultant explained that: "it is very new rhetoric, it's a new way of presenting things in the UN. You

---

[13] See Scheyvens et al. (2016, pp. 374–375) for a discussion of private-sector involvement in the SDG processes.

couldn't say just five, ten years ago that it is actually ok to earn money on sustainability, that it is ok to earn money on the poor" (field notes, Denmark, May 2019). He was part of a program that assisted small- and medium-sized industrial Danish companies with developing new products, and helped the businesses translate SDGs into profitable opportunities. At the same event, a consultant for a large confederation of Danish private-sector employers exclaimed that one of the reasons the confederation cared about the SDGs is that delivering the SDGs could generate business opportunities valued at 12 trillion dollars. While he was a bit critical toward the exact number, he joked that "a lot of the money ... is going to be paid to sustainability consultants, like myself," making the audience laugh (field notes, Denmark, May 2019).

A focus on sustainability, climate change and development thus presents opportunities to make money while helping businesses to "mitigate reputational risk, add to the bottom line, create new product lines, enhance brand loyalty, and increase their power" (Ponte 2019, p. 14). Yet, the combination of doing good and profit-making is pursued not only as part of "capital's never-ending search to accumulate, a process driven by shadowy, unspecified capitalist elites with singular interests," it also involves "a different and diverse set of actors, institutions, and driving rationalities" (Dempsey 2016, p. 15). It is easy to become misled when attending events where one is surrounded by professional salespeople who know how to stay on their narrative message; however, there was some indication that certain companies and individuals were as concerned with sustainability as they were with profit. They encouraged other businesses to learn from them, and even made their key research findings or other outputs open source. When this became apparent during presentations, the audience would applaud enthusiastically. There were even presenters indicating the possibility of a new capitalist system, with one exclaiming that since the economy "is being designed, then it can be redesigned!" (field notes, Denmark, November 2017). As one presenter proclaimed:

> *A common narrative ... [was] that business was the enemy and that NGOs and governments were gonna save us. And I just really passionately felt that there were as many good people working inside business as there are in governments and NGOs.* (Field notes, Denmark, October 2017)

For-Profit Hero Metanarratives: We Could All Be Heroes

When comparing the long-standing development hero metanarratives and the for-profit hero metanarratives emerging at the events I attended, some differences in the structure and storyline can be seen. One of the defining features of the development hero metanarratives is that the "distant other in need" plays a vital role in justifying interventions and encouraging donations. In the for-profit hero metanarratives, however, the distant other plays a less visible role and may even have become a potential "market to be served" or "business opportunity, rather than Others to be helped" (Menga & Goodman 2022, p. 722). This has consequences for how challenges pertaining to sustainability, climate change and development are conceptualized and solutions operationalized.

While focusing less on the victims, the for-profit hero metanarratives that I encountered included heroes and villains similar to those found in long-standing development hero metanarratives. The importance of these characters was even taught at the previously mentioned workshop, held by a British communications agency, on how businesses can create stories that get support, commitment and resources. The presenters explained – inspired by Joseph Campbell (Campbell 1949), an influential professor of literature and comparative mythology – that a good story has eight elements:

1) "Everyday hero"
2) "Ordinary world"
3) "Compelling villain"
4) "Call to adventure"
5) "Crossing the threshold"
6) "Three challenges"
7) "Mentors, allies and gifts"
8) "Return with the elixir"

The compelling villain must be tangible, they clarified. They gave the example that climate change is too vague a category, instead someone burning plastic to keep warm is a better villain. Blaming local practices, such as burning plastic, for causing environmental destruction is in line with development hero metanarratives. However, the distant other in need as *victim* no longer, as noted, seemed to play a central role. Instead, a "nearby sustainability superhero," such as a sustainability-minded consumer, employee, shareholder or company founder, had become a key actor in the story. This actor, as I will show, does not need a distant victim to perform heroic acts of sustainability. Other research on conservation and climate change mitigation has similarly shown that fusing profit-making and nature protection often goes hand-in-hand with a focus on the individual – such as the innovative entrepreneur, the famous celebrity or the affluent consumer – as opposed to societal factors (Brockington 2009; Dempsey 2016; Igoe 2017; Lekakis 2012; Prudham 2009). This accords well with "liberal rationales of improvement" that economic incentives will induce the individual to do good via the market (Dempsey 2016, p. 7). For example, paying someone not to cut down a tree is perceived as a solution to deforestation that does not necessitate engaging with "messy politics and social relations" (Dempsey 2016, p. 8).

Figure 8 Workshop on how to tell a good story, held by consultants for businesses. Denmark, October 2017. Photo by author.

The consultants hosting the workshop on how to tell a good story encouraged the audience to include themselves as a hero in a convincing for-profit narrative of doing good even though it might feel a bit awkward to do so (see Figure 8). This was because:

> *It is really hard for someone to care about the success of someone or something if they know nothing about them ... It is one of the [narrative] elements that sometimes people forget, and this works for an organization as well. Why are you trying to make this change, why are you going on this journey?* (Field notes, Denmark, October 2017)

At different events, I heard several presenters begin their presentation by recounting their own "hero's journey." They would usually begin by describing how they discovered a problem or crisis and then heroically worked out a solution that would form the basis for the business endeavor. Geographer Scott Prudham (2009), writing on green capitalism, argues that the heroic entrepreneur may serve a greater purpose than merely engaging the spectator.

Green capitalism is an example of the merging of profit-making and doing good, in this case, environmentalism and capitalism, which could easily be otherwise perceived as being in opposition. In capitalism, the key actor is the capitalist entrepreneur whose innovative dynamism is driven by a desire for capital accumulation (Prudham 2009, p. 1603). To fuse environmentalism and capitalism, this actor "must be seen – in political and cultural terms – to be an architect of, rather than an obstacle to, a greener future" (Prudham 2009, p. 1605). He explains that this is achieved by entrepreneurial elites "performing" green capitalism "as a sort of 'drama'" in which the entrepreneur takes on the role of environmental crusader "harnessing capital investment, individual choice, and entrepreneurial innovation to the green cause" (Prudham 2009, pp. 1595–1596; see also Christiansen & Olwig 2019).

Another important potential hero category is the employee, and this version of the "good story" is very much linked to internal communication within the business. While the presenters at the events I attended were proud of their achievements in doing and promoting good, they also discussed the difficulties of convincing colleagues in their respective businesses of the "value of values," and presenters would swap tips on how best to persuade colleagues that doing good is good for branding and business. One argument used for such persuasion was that a purpose-led company would get better employees who would be more likely to stay. Businesses were therefore finding ways to instill a culture of heroicness (cf. Ho 2009) among their staff. Thus, on the first day of a three-day conference, the following showed up on my conference app: "Are you ready to release your inner superhero? ... join us Oct 31st at 8am to explore the 5 Powers of a Sustainability Superhero" (field notes, Denmark, October 2017). This turned out to be an advertisement for an event on how to make employees feel like superheroes. I decided to go to it. During this event, we were first asked to pose as our favorite superhero because "people learn best through games." I happened to be sitting next to a woman who showed me an app she was working on for a different company that was doing exactly the same thing. She was attending this event to get inspiration for how to improve their app.

Other presenters discussed how working for a better cause made them feel happier and heroic, and at one of the events, there was also a book for sale that included the term "happy hero" in the title. The book inspired presenters to use this phrase, as exemplified by the presenter from a sustainable hair care line who explained that he joined the beauty industry:

> *For beautiful models, glamorous shots, traveling around the world. And ...*
> *it's funny, and it's really real, because today talking about Cradle-to-Cradle*

> *certifications, being able to say my whole production is 100% PCR [post-consumer resin], or 100% solar energy, I'm happier, I'm prouder, I'm more fulfilled. So ... I'm a very happy, happy hero.* (Field notes, Denmark, October 2017)

In fact, "feeling good," both as a consumer, CEO and employee, emanated from the whole event, which had as its overarching theme "redefining the good life." This is apparent in my field notes describing the lively atmosphere I encountered upon entering an enormous, festively lit plenary room:

> *There is a DJ playing music and I feel like I am going clubbing. There are several round tables and some rows of chairs. People are chit chatting happily. I guess this conference really is focused on the good life ... We're all asked to answer an online survey on our phones regarding what defines the good life for us. Our answers appear on the screen as we write. "Happiness" wins.* (Field notes, Denmark, October 2017)

Through such spectacle, the organizers design and structure the spaces of the conferences in such a way that they can promote certain kinds of interaction, and legitimize and transmit specific forms of knowledge (MacDonald 2010, p. 262). Such spaces increasingly extend into the virtual through the use of, for example, conference apps, tags and hashtags (see Figure 9).

In my research, I also found several examples where the consumer was the hero in the story, and the role of the business was to be an inspiring motivator. In other words, the consumer is no longer a distant viewer who can only relate to the situation portrayed through a distant heroic NGO. Now it is the consumer who performs the heroic acts nearby. As the executive director of a certification label explained in a presentation, 40 percent of consumers fall into the category that she referred to as the aspirational consumer, or "aspirationals," a category that cuts across class, race and social position. According to this presenter, "It's no longer about asking consumers to buy something. It's about inspiring them to be something by helping them reveal their best selves and realize a better world" (field notes, Denmark, October 2017). This appears to be the latest version of what Igoe describes as a mass-marketing culture in which commodities "seem to possess impossible powers, for example, a luxury watch can enhance our passion and love ... [T]hese claims now extend to the possibilities of making a better world" (Igoe 2017, p. 93). This leads to more consumption instead of the consumer doing good by, for example, boycotting certain products (Igoe 2017, p. 33). Combined with social media, consumers can become "mini-celebrities," using their heroic acts of consumption in order to "brand and market" their "virtual personas" (Igoe 2017, p. 96; see also Olwig & Christiansen 2016).

Figure 9 A conference app can be part of structuring the conference space. Denmark, October 2017.

Similarly, "the purpose" can be the hero. As the presenter from the sustainable hair care line said: "we started making that purpose more of the hero than the product itself." The manufacturing of the sustainable hair care line, only one of the company's many lines of hair care, experienced difficulties because it could only use natural ingredients. These, as opposed to synthetic ingredients, were not consistent, and the bottles made from PCR had a grey color. The presenter explained, "I have to admit, when we started this, we had absolutely no idea of exactly what we were doing, where we were going, how far we were going to go on this project," but added that they found solutions, such as "choosing beautiful grey colors." The presenter called for the audience to "join the [name of hair care line][14] movement" and explained that this movement was why he still worked for the company:

---

[14] I have chosen to anonymize quotes, primarily because the goal of this analysis is not to single out companies, but rather to identify more overarching narratives.

> *So, today, all hundreds of you here, when you go back to your hotel, tonight, tomorrow morning, when you step in that shower, promise to help ... Stop your shower maybe 10–20 seconds shorter than the one you did yesterday and try doing that every day. Do shower though! [Laughter] ... Each one of us can have an impact.* (Field notes, Denmark, October 2017)

In this way, the product is no longer part of, or only supporting, an environmental or social movement, but becomes the movement itself.

In relation to the storyline, the key change from the long-standing development hero metanarratives is that for-profit hero metanarratives often have a stronger focus on the journey itself than on the end of the story. Having an end (in the sense of reaching a clearly defined objective) is important within the development sector in order to monitor and evaluate projects, and to prove to donors that the NGOs deserve future funding. The for-profit hero metanarrative, however, seems to be an endless journey. Furthermore, it is even good for the story to include failure. As explained by the consultants from the workshop on how to tell a good story: "we love jeopardy, we love struggle ... if it was easy for them [the hero] we kinda lose interest ... we love building up a hero, we love knocking them down again." Later they elaborated: "hopefully, by taking someone on this journey, you make the challenges seem big, and pretty hard to tackle, so it is understandable that you cannot solve them overnight" (field notes, Denmark, October 2017).

While for-profits also have to monitor and evaluate for the sake of their investors, their timeline is different from that of NGOs that have to work from project to project. The for-profits need to show ongoing progress and improvement in relation to their products, and this fits into the idea of a journey. The concept of "a journey" was used often in the presentations, and many also referred to various hardships and difficulties such as the need to learn, make mistakes, not be perfect and be selective in relation to the SDGs, as illustrated in the following quotes: "The partnerships for us have been a journey, we have learned a lot from the partnerships, and I think there is a lot of room for improvement in the future" (field notes, Denmark, March 2018); "one thing is for sure, we don't have all the answers quite yet" (field notes, Denmark, October 2017); "we are not perfect, but we are trying to get better" (field notes, Denmark, October 2017); "you won't see all 17 goals in our strategy, but you will see some key goals" (field notes, Denmark, October 2017). On the one hand, a focus on the journey and the difficulties it may entail could lead to more transparency and honesty. On the other hand, it could also provide an easy way to avoid taking responsibility and being held accountable for the impact and result of the journey, giving businesses an excuse for only addressing certain goals and ignoring others, and giving consumers an excuse to only focus on small everyday acts – such as shampooing.

While the "needy victim" category in long-standing development hero meta-narratives problematically takes away agency from imagined beneficiaries who, it is implied, must be "saved" in order to alleviate their suffering (e.g., Ferguson 1994; Maren 1997; Pruce 2016), the "hero" category in for-profit hero meta-narratives is equally questionable. These heroes are celebrated for doing good by supporting commercial initiatives through investments, employment or consumption anywhere. The hero category thus encourages actors to put themselves into the picture, but by foregrounding their own reflection, these heroes simultaneously are distracted from focusing on the broader historical-geographical structural issues. As will be discussed in the next subsection, important context-specific structural inequalities are also obfuscated because for-profit development hero narratives reinforce universalistic development logics through integrating these logics with global business management logics.

Universalizing Management Logics versus Context-Specific Structural Inequalities

The SDGs universalized the world's problems into goals and targets that could be tracked, measured and managed in accounting terms. This is a continuation of a larger trend by which civil society and government organizations have increasingly become subject to management strategies and logics typically identified with business (Davis et al. 2012; Fukuda-Parr & McNeill 2019; Gladwell 2002; Ho 2009; McKenna 2006). An important dimension of tracking performance according to this business-oriented management logic is that success is reduced to reaching a certain number. In relation to the SDGs, this "requires simplification of complex ideas into a set of measurable common elements, abstraction from diverse local settings, and reification of intangible social phenomena" (Fukuda-Parr & McNeill 2019, p. 7).

Such "governance by indicators" (Davis et al. 2012) leads to a dependence on "experts to determine how to convert concepts into readily countable form" (Merry 2019, p. 146). The same (management) experts are used in different types of organizations, whether for-profit or non-profit, public or private, national or international. This is in part a result of the private governance logic of New Public Management. For NGOs this "has further consolidated an audits-and-ratings NGO culture that shapes the orientation of the sector less towards public and non-profit logics and more towards social impact metrics and performance indicators" (Chouliaraki & Vestergaard 2022, p. 5).

Another consequence is that by reducing complex ideas to a number, and thereby translating local diversity into generic abstraction, the indicators used to measure success are considered to be universally applicable, as in the case of the

SDGs. Yet, by governing the SDGs through universal indicators, it appears to become inconsequential whether a challenge is related to development, sustainability or climate change, and whether it is found in one location or another. Such universalizing management logics obfuscate context-specific structural inequalities, and the postcolonial economic and social power relations that characterize interactions in particular places (e.g., Büscher 2019; Fukuda-Parr 2016; Fukuda-Parr & McNeill 2019; Mawdsley 2018).

Section 4 showed how long-standing development hero metanarratives are converging with influential climate change metanarratives. With the SDGs, development, sustainability and climate change were subsumed under the broad category of sustainable development. This section has demonstrated how the SDGs were then subsequently inscribed in emerging for-profit hero metanarratives that involve everyday sustainability superheroes anywhere and everywhere. As has been seen, the growing role of the private sector in sustainable development was in part driven by businesses' concern with redefining doing good in a way that enables, rather than challenges, making a profit and building a positive brand. On the other hand, involving for-profits in doing good has also been used by non-profits and other actors, including for-profit actors, as a tactic to gain access to new resources and, alternatively, as a way to change things from the inside and making doing good the profitable thing to do. While these various actors are motivated by different ideologies and rationalities to make doing good "visible and economically legible" (Dempsey 2016, p. 12), the end result is that they give hegemonic power to the idea that profit-making and doing good are compatible, or even co-dependent.

6 Conclusion: Mobilizing Grounded Stories

The single story creates stereotypes. And the problem with stereotypes is not that they are untrue, but that they are incomplete. They make one story become the only story ... Stories matter. Many stories matter. Stories have been used to dispossess and to malign. But stories can also be used to empower, and to humanize. Stories can break the dignity of a people. But stories can also repair that broken dignity.
– Chimamanda Ngozi Adichie (2009)

As the influential Nigerian author Chimamanda Ngozi Adichie puts it in her 2009 TED talk cited here, stories are powerful, and stories can become problematically powerful, when they become too dominant. *A Bit Too Simple* has investigated powerful and problematic storylines that villainize local populations by blaming them for causing decline and environmental destruction, and heroize external aid workers by presenting them as coming to the rescue. By focusing on these problematic storylines, referred to here as development hero metanarratives, this Element has uncovered how, why and to what effect they have become such a dominant force in driving international action, even when more grounded narratives tell stories that differ. This Element has further shown that these influential metanarratives are converging with sustainability and climate change narratives over time, space and sectors and explored these globalized narratives and their relationship with varying actors and the choices they make.

This Element has shown that taking a point of departure in a simplified crisis, reducing complexity, standardizing storylines and building on generically familiar plots and the well-known characters of the villains, victims and heroes are all key components in convincing narratives. Furthermore, such narratives often draw on religious and mythical narratives, as was exemplified by examining development hero metanarratives of decline and environmental destruction. Section 2 discussed how the narrative element of flooding as a crisis and divine punishment can be linked to ancient religious texts, and Section 3 pointed out how the "declensionist" plot of destructive human behavior resulting in nature's decline (or declension) is tied to the story of Adam and Eve's expulsion from Eden. Section 4 demonstrated how this declensionist plot continues to frame climate change solutions today. Finally, Section 5 gave the example of how the eight key elements of narratives presented to a group of businesspeople for the purpose of telling a "good story" about their own "hero's journey" in solving sustainability challenges derived from an academic textbook (Campbell 1949) that draws on comparative mythology in the study of literature. These religious and mythic narratives and elements, however, have no clear origin in-so-far as they can be found in many different sources going back through the ages, and they continue to influence storytelling and the discourses informed by these narratives up to the present, even in the world of business. Thus, even if one cannot identify the origin of a narrative, one can recognize a narrative by the fact that the same basic storyline or plot keeps reappearing. And because this basic storyline is used and reused, it seems familiar and therefore convincing.

Development hero metanarratives have had serious consequences. As Adichie states, such dominant metanarratives can break the dignity of a people. I have here shown that they can also contribute to breaking their environments and their livelihoods. Indeed, this Element has illustrated how these metanarratives hold such hegemonic power that they can become internalized by the actors involved and impact their practices. Being continually presented as victims who need to be saved from their own "villainous" behavior toward the environment can, for example, induce local people to question the validity of their own understandings of environmental challenges and how to address these challenges. In northern Ghana, we thus saw how a dominant desertification narrative misleadingly presented the local population as causing the desert to spread through local resource mismanagement. This led to a dominant narrative on the need for external practitioners to teach the local population how to change their behavior – even in times of flooding that was clearly aggravated by broader environmental and geopolitical challenges. For example, when an upstream dam located in Burkina Faso was unable to handle the large amount of rain, it resulted in flooding downstream. Yet, rather than introducing and discussing flood management planning, conversations among practitioners and local populations alike continued to revolve around the need to change local behavior downstream to avoid desertification. The continual emphasis on problematic local behavior can be traced to colonial transformations of subjectivity that combine a heroization of the colonial presence with an internalization of inferiority among the local population, eventually generating desires for outmigration (Fanon 1967; Leach & Mearns 1996; Salazar 2011; Sen 2020a; Sultana 2022). Such dominating metanarratives thus obstruct constructive solutions.

These metanarratives also influence the external development actor, who is presented as playing the role of the hero. The external development interventions are thereby not only justified but perceived as essential for saving the local people and, with the advent of climate change, even the planet. Compounded by the element of crisis, and the associated sense of urgency, these metanarratives impede the critical questioning of such interventions and their potential negative consequences. This was seen in the case of Vietnam where the phenomenon of seasonal flooding was reimagined as a new crisis caused by global climate change, even though livelihoods in this part of Vietnam depended on periodic flooding. This is particularly problematic if interventions only focus on preventing flooding, as a lack of flooding would be detrimental to local livelihoods. Furthermore, politically contentious technocratic modernization strategies, such as urbanization through relocating of villages, could be reframed as moving villages away from flooding, and thereby justified as flood protection measures. Finally, the simplified crisis storyline on global climate change–induced flooding distracted from state-led infrastructure, such as hydropower plants and commercial forest plantations that problematically impacted seasonal flooding flows and patterns.

The metanarratives of development, sustainability and climate change discussed throughout the Element simplified and articulated challenges through the application of universalistic and technocratic management rationalities, which effectively amount to an "anti-politics machine" that makes politically loaded environmental challenges appear to be solvable through technical solutions (Ferguson 1994). Such solutions gloss over or even reinforce inequalities, thereby maintaining a geopolitical status quo. This anti-politics machine has, for example, led to a plethora of initiatives focused on tree planting in the Global South as a universalistic and technocratic, yet also natural, salvational solution to climate change. These interventions are furthermore justified as means for "civilizing" local forest management. However, as the cases from southern Ghana and Tanzania have shown, a tree is not simply a tree, and undifferentiated tree planting can be bad for people, the environment and the planet. Most prominent among these initiatives is REDD+, the UN's primary mechanism for supporting climate change mitigation, which is premised on the familiar long-standing development story that "heroic" external actors are needed to "save" the local population in "developing countries" – and the planet – by teaching them the errors of their ways. In the words of the UN, the REDD+ program needs to "incentivize" the local people (UN-REDD Programme 2016). We thus see how contemporary narratives on climate change follow a storyline similar to long-standing development hero metanarratives, thereby resulting in a converging effect between narratives. This converging effect reinforces the status quo in geopolitical power relations and local living conditions, and it has even led to further inequalities and inefficiencies in the transition toward sustainability and well-being.

The ethnographic cases presented in this Element clearly show "the danger of a single story," as Adichie's 2009 TED talk was entitled. Many hegemonizing development narratives have problematically become so dominant that they are perceived as conventional wisdom and have become part of many actors' habitus – be they donors, local administrators, practitioners, recipients or for-profits. This is in part because, as demonstrated throughout the Element, these metanarratives have been so effective at creating an overriding universalistic order bridging the worlds of actors in different geographical locations and positions in relation to the development sector, scientists from different fields and, increasingly, the business sector. The SDGs furthered this process because sustainable development challenges worldwide were translated into (Eurocentric) universalistic goals and indicators that can be measured and governed through numbers with a little help from consultants (Davis et al. 2012; Fukuda-Parr & McNeill 2019; Merry 2019). The SDGs' focus on seemingly universalist goals and objectively measurable numbers obscured the politics, theories and values of the framework and the choice of particular measurement tools and goals (Fukuda-Parr & Muchhala 2020, p. 7). In addition, by turning development, sustainability and climate change into challenges that could be quantified and tackled through business-like management, and by centering the role of for-profits in reaching the goals, the SDGs further institutionalized the notion that profit-making and doing good involve symbiotic rather than competing rationalities.

As stated in the Introduction, translating scientific results into policy and practice will by necessity often involve simplifying complexity, and narratives can play a key role in this regard. Familiar storylines can facilitate action in the face of complex challenges, such as climate change. Narratives play an important role in how different actor categories understand and choose to react to challenges. Yet, if the stories are hegemonizing as overarching metanarratives, they may from the perspective of local populations in both the Global North and South, lead to only action, not agency in the sense of being able to exercise an informed choice and act accordingly. Moreover, the successful exposing of the fallacy of such hegemonizing narratives, and the kind of development projects they have generated, may only result in even greater disillusionment and counterproductive action.

Dominant metanarratives cannot simply be challenged and deconstructed using a social, applied or natural science perspective. While there will always be a drive towards universalistic cookie-cutter approach solutions, it is possible to develop more complex and place-specific understandings of challenges by listening to differing stories, *many* stories, and in particular grounded stories. As Sultana (2022, p. 9) argues, such stories must be included in mainstream discourse and practice, thereby moving from universality to pluriversality (see also Escobar 2018; Kothari et al. 2019; Paulson 2019). By this she means that "to redress ongoing oppressions and marginalizations" (Sultana 2002, p. 6) it is necessary: "to make visible and draw attention to knowledges and lived experiences otherwise, to ground theory in places geographically and ontologically, to emplace theory in concrete struggles that recognize various forms of resistance to domination" (Sultana 2002, p. 9). Following Adichie, these stories can repair the dignity of people that has been undermined by the single story. They do so not only by being less Eurocentric, but also by becoming more inclusive and potentially less alienating. As Mutua explains, "it is important to note that the terms 'European' or 'Eurocentric' are used descriptively and do not necessarily connote evil or undesirability. They do, however, point to notions of cultural specificity and historical exclusivity" (Mutua 2001, p. 204).

It is not enough to make room for, and acknowledge, multiple local stories. It is necessary to actively seek out a variety of different stories to mobilize them in the context of climate change and development. There are examples around the world of local stories successfully being mobilized and sometimes even being taken up by large institutions and incorporated into policymaking. This is exemplified by the climate justice movement, youth climate activist movements such as Fridays for the Future, the degrowth movement, Indigenous activist movements and the "loss and damages" campaign. The loss and damages campaign even spurred the establishment of the Loss and Damage Fund in connection with the 27th COP to the UNFCCC (COP27). The importance of the campaign was acknowledged in the UN News: "Developing countries made strong and repeated appeals for the establishment of a loss and damage fund, to compensate the countries that are the most vulnerable to climate disasters, yet who have contributed little to the climate crisis" (Wilhelmova 2022).

By showing how hegemonizing narratives clash with lived reality, this Element has endeavored to reveal a multiplicity of storylines. Drawing on different ethnographic methods, including participant observation, online, insider and event ethnography, fieldwork in multiple sites and interviews with actors at different levels of the development sector, it has presented different actors' stories. In Vietnam, I thus heard stories of how mice and insects destroyed the crops if there were no floods. I also heard stories of villagers who were happy when the floods came because this meant they could go fishing and earn money. Water is clearly integral to a Vietnamese way of life (see Figure 10). But flooding was not always good, and I heard stories about how

Figure 10 In theater, text and landscape scenery complement one another in communicating a narrative. The ancient Vietnamese folk tradition of using water as the stage for narrative performance thus tells much about the degree to which water is integral to a Vietnamese way of life, cultivating rice, using water buffalo and catching fish, in which flooding is part of the flow of existence. Water puppetry was originally performed in flooded rice patties. This photo, by the author, is from the Thang Long Water Puppet Theater in Hanoi, Vietnam, January 2005.

technocratic interventions, such as hydropower plants, disrupted hydrological flows. Floods thus come in many shapes and sizes, some of which are absolutely crucial to maintaining a livelihood.

In Ghana and Tanzania, I heard stories about how some trees were good for shade, some for fruits and some for timber, and that the environmental and socioeconomic benefit of trees changed depending on the age and location of the tree. I also heard stories about trees that required too many nutrients or absorbed too much water and therefore negatively impacted the local ecosystem. Trees, just like floods, come in different shapes and sizes, and to understand the impact of trees in specific locations, we need grounded stories. It is on the basis of such grounded stories that research is emerging that illuminates the teleconnections of local outcomes with far flung processes, actions, and relationships; which establishes local populations have agency and important knowledge of local resource management; which shows how undifferentiated tree planting is not a good climate solution, and that nature-based solutions more broadly can be problematic; which uncovers how commercial forest plantations and monocultures lead to loss or decline of biodiversity and support the external appropriation of funds; and which demonstrates that the SDGs are a mismatch of competing goals of governments and different UN agencies.

Grounded stories can form the basis for a different form of agency that can be more forceful and productive for local populations, leading to localized understandings of problems and solutions. Climate change and sustainability challenges are serious and complex, and as this Element has shown, a multiplicity of narratives and discourses can reveal where and how especially dominant metanarratives are "a bit too simple." By actively seeking out and listening to these stories, policy, practice and action can be better informed and made more valuable because they are grounded in lived realities rather than abstract global imaginaries.

References

Adger, W. N., Benjaminsen, T. A., Brown, K., & Svarstad, H. (2001). Advancing a Political Ecology of Global Environmental Discourses. *Development and Change*, **32**(4), 681–715.

Adger, W. N., Eakin, H., & Winkels, A. (2009). Nested and Teleconnected Vulnerabilities to Environmental Change. *Frontiers in Ecology and the Environment*, **7**(3), 150–157.

Adichie, C. N. (2009). *The Danger of a Single Story*, presented at the TEDGlobal. Retrieved from www.ted.com/talks/chimamanda_ngozi_adichie_the_danger_of_a_single_story/comment (accessed June 30, 2025).

Agrawal, A. (1995). Dismantling the Divide between Indigenous and Scientific Knowledge. *Development and Change*, **26**(3), 413–439.

Apthorpe, R. (2011). Coda: With Alice in Aidland: A Seriously Satirical Allegory. In D. Mosse, ed., *Adventures in Aidland: The Anthropology of Professionals in International Development*, New York: Berghahn Books, pp. 1–31.

Arnall, A., & Kothari, U. (2015). Challenging Climate Change and Migration Discourse: Different Understandings of Timescale and Temporality in the Maldives. *Global Environmental Change*, **31**, 199–206.

Arnall, A., Kothari, U., & Kelman, I. (2014). Introduction to Politics of Climate Change: Discourses of Policy and Practice in Developing Countries . *The Geographical Journal*, **180**(2), 98–101.

Ascough, H. (2018). Once Upon a Time: Using the Hero's Journey in Development Stories. *Canadian Journal of Development Studies/Revue Canadienne d'études Du Développement*, **39**(4), 533–549.

Asiyanbi, A., & Lund, J. (2020). Policy Persistence: REDD+ between Stabilization and Contestation. *Journal of Political Ecology*, **27**(1), 378–400. http://dx.doi.org/10.2458/v27i1.23493.

Bankoff, G., Frerks, G., & Hilhorst, T., eds. (2004). *Mapping Vulnerability: Disasters, Development, and People*, London: Earthscan Publications.

Batterbury, S., & Warren, A. (2001). Desertification. In *International Encyclopedia of the Social & Behavioral Sciences*, Amsterdam: Elsevier, pp. 3526–3529. https://doi.org/10.1016/B0-08-043076-7/04172-3.

Bebbington, A., Guggenheim, S., Olson, E., & Woolcock, M. (2004). Exploring Social Capital Debates at the World Bank. *Journal of Development Studies*, **40**(5), 33–64.

Benjaminsen, T. A. (2021). Depicting Decline: Images and Myths in Environmental Discourse Analysis. *Landscape Research*, **46**(2), 211–225.

Bhambra, G. K. (2009). Postcolonial Europe, or Understanding Europe in Times of the Postcolonial. In C. Rumford, ed., *The SAGE Handbook of European Studies*, London: SAGE Publications Ltd., pp. 69–86. http://dx.doi.org/10.4135/9780857021045.

Bierschenk, T., Chauveau, J.-P., & Olivier de Sardan, J.-P. (2002). *Local Development Brokers in Africa: The Rise of a New Social Category*, Mainz: Institut für Ethnologie und Afrikastudien. Working Paper, no. 13.

Boadi, S. A., Bosselman, A. S., Owusu, K., Asare, R., & Olwig, M. F. (2024). Household Economics of Cocoa Agroforestry: Costs and Benefits. In M. F. Olwig, A. S. Bosselman, & K. Owusu, eds., *Agroforestry as Climate Change Adaptation: The Case of Cocoa Farming in Ghana*, London: Palgrave Macmillan, pp. 121–145. https://doi.org/10.1007/978-3-031-45635-0_5.

Bond, W. J., Stevens, N., Midgley, G. F., & Lehmann, C. E. R. (2019). The Trouble with Trees: Afforestation Plans for Africa. *Trends in Ecology & Evolution*, **34**(11), 963–965. https://doi.org/10.1016/j.tree.2019.08.003.

Boserup, E. (1965). *The Conditions of Agricultural Growth: The Economics of Agrarian Change under Population Pressure*, London: George Allen & Unwin.

Bosselman, A. S., Boadi, S. A., Olwig, M. F., & Asare, R. (2024). Social Challenges and Opportunities in Agroforestry: Cocoa Farmers' Perspectives. In M. F. Olwig, A. S. Bosselman, & K. Owusu, eds., *Agroforestry as Climate Change Adaptation: The Case of Cocoa Farming in Ghana*, London: Palgrave Macmillan, pp. 93–119. https://doi.org/10.1007/978-3-031-45635-0_4.

Brockington, D. (2002). *Fortress Conservation: The Preservation of the Mkomazi Game Reserve, Tanzania*, Oxford: James Currey.

Brockington, D. (2009). *Celebrity and the Environment: Fame, Wealth and Power in Conservation*, London: Zed Books.

Brogaard, L., & Petersen, O. H. (2018). Public–Private Partnerships (PPPs) in Development Policy: Exploring the Concept and Practice. *Development Policy Review*, **36**, O729–O747.

Brundtland, G. H. (1987). *Our Common Future: Report of the World Commission on Environment and Development*. Geneva: United Nations. Dokument A/42/427. Retrieved from http://www.un-documents.net/ocf-ov.htm.

Bruner, E. M. (1986). Ethnography as Narrative. In V. W. Turner & E. M. Bruner, eds., *The Anthropology of Experience*, Urbana: University of Illinois Press, pp. 139–155.

Bruun, O. (2012). Sending the Right Bill to the Right People: Climate Change, Environmental Degradation, and Social Vulnerabilities in Central Vietnam. *Weather, Climate, and Society,* **4**(4), 250–262.

Bruun, O., & Olwig, M. F. (2015). Is Local Community the Answer?: The Role of "Local Knowledge" and "Community" for Disaster Prevention and Climate Adaptation in Central Vietnam. *Asian Journal of Social Science,* **43**(6), 811–836. https://doi.org/10.1163/15685314-04306008.

Bruun, T. B., Ryan, C. M., de Neergaard, A., & Berry, N. J. (2021). Soil Organic Carbon Stocks Maintained Despite Intensification of Shifting Cultivation. *Geoderma,* **388**, 114804.

Budabin, A. C., & Richey, L. A. (2018). Advocacy Narratives and Celebrity Engagement: The Case of Ben Affleck in Congo. *Human Rights Quarterly,* **40**(2), 260–286.

Budabin, A. C., & Richey, L. A. (2021). *Batman Saves the Congo: How Celebrities Disrupt the Politics of Development,* Minneapolis: University of Minnesota Press.

Büscher, B. (2019). From "Global" to "Revolutionary" Development. *Development and Change,* **50**(2), 484–494.

Büscher, B. (2021). *The Truth about Nature: Environmentalism in the Era of Post-truth Politics and Platform Capitalism,* Oakland: University of California Press.

Cameron, J. D., Solomon, E., & Clarke, W. (2022). Soundtracks of Poverty and Development: Music, Emotions and Representations of the Global South. *The European Journal of Development Research,* **34**(2), 785–805.

Campbell, J. (1949). *The Hero with a Thousand Faces,* New York: Pantheon Books.

Campbell, L. M., Corson, C., Gray, N. J., MacDonald, K. I., & Brosius, J. P. (2014). Studying Global Environmental Meetings to Understand Global Environmental Governance: Collaborative Event Ethnography at the Tenth Conference of the Parties to the Convention on Biological Diversity. *Global Environmental Politics,* **14**(3), 1–20.

Castree, N., Adams, W. M., Barry, J., ... Wynne, B. (2014). Changing the Intellectual Climate. *Nature Climate Change,* **4**(9), 763–768.

Charney, J., Stone, P. H., & Quirk, W. J. (1975). Drought in the Sahara: A Biogeophysical Feedback Mechanism. *Science,* **187**(4175), 434–435.

Chouliaraki, L. (2006). *The Spectatorship of Suffering,* London: SAGE Publications Ltd.

Chouliaraki, L. (2013). *The Ironic Spectator: Solidarity in the Age of Post-humanitarianism,* Cambridge: Polity.

Chouliaraki, L., & Vestergaard, A. (2022). Introduction: Humanitarian Communication in the 21st Century. In L. Chouliaraki & A. Vestergaard, eds., *Routledge Handbook of Humanitarian Communication*, Abingdon: Routledge, pp. 1–22.

Christiansen, L. B., & Olwig, M. F. (2019). The Corporate Karma Carnival: Offline and Online Games, Branding and Humanitarianism at Roskilde Festival. In R. Tavernor & M. Lawrence, eds., *Global Humanitarianism and Media Culture*, Manchester: Manchester University Press, pp. 246–267. https://doi.org/10.7765/9781526117304.00022.

Colten, C. E. (2009). *Perilous Place, Powerful Storms: Hurricane Protection in Coastal Louisiana*, Jackson: University Press of Mississippi.

Danielsen, F., Sørensen, M. K., Olwig, M. F., ... Suryadiputra, N. (2005). The Asian Tsunami: A Protective Role for Coastal Vegetation. *Science*, **310** (5748), 643–643. https://doi.org/10.1126/science.1118387.

Davis, K. E., Fisher, A., Kingsbury, B., & Merry, S., E. (2012). *Governance by Indicators: Global Power through Quantification and Rankings*, Oxford: Oxford University Press [in association with Institute for International Law and Justice, New York University School of Law].

Dempsey, J. (2016). *Enterprising Nature: Economics, Markets, and Finance in Global Biodiversity Politics*, Chichester: John Wiley & Sons.

Engberg-Pedersen, L., & Fejerskov, A. M. (2018). The Transformation of Danish Foreign Aid. In K. Fischer & H. Mouritzen, eds., *Danish Foreign Policy Review 2018*, Copenhagen: Danish Institute for International Studies.

Escobar, A. (1995). *Encountering Development: The Making and Unmaking of the Third World*, Princeton, NJ: Princeton University Press.

Escobar, A. (2018). *Designs for the Pluriverse: Radical Interdependence, Autonomy, and the Making of Worlds*, Durham, NC: Duke University Press. http://dx.doi.org/10.1215/9780822371816.

Fadlalla, A. H. (2019). *Branding Humanity: Competing Narratives of Rights, Violence, and Global Citizenship*, Stanford, CA: Stanford University Press.

Fairbank, M. (2019, December 2). Tree Plantations – The Good, the Bad and the Ugly. *Paper Advance: News for the Paper Industry Professional*.

Falck, O., & Heblich, S. (2007). Corporate Social Responsibility: Doing Well by Doing Good. *Business Horizons*, **50**(3), 247–254.

Fanon, F. (1967). *Black Skin White Masks*, New York: Grove Press.

Fensholt, R., Langanke, T., Rasmussen, K., ... Wessels, K. (2012). Greenness in Semi-arid Areas across the Globe 1981–2007: An Earth Observing Satellite Based Analysis of Trends and Drivers. *Remote Sensing of Environment*, **121**, 144–158.

Ferguson, J. (1994). *The Anti-politics Machine: "Development," Depoliticization and Bureaucratic Power in Lesotho*, Minneapolis: University of Minnesota Press.

Fischer, K., Giertta, F., & Hajdu, F. (2019). Carbon-Binding Biomass or a Diversity of Useful Trees? (Counter)topographies of Carbon Forestry in Uganda. *Environment and Planning E: Nature and Space*, **2**(1), 178–199.

Fischer, K., & Hajdu, F. (2018). The Importance of the Will to Improve: How "Sustainability" Sidelined Local Livelihoods in a Carbon-Forestry Investment in Uganda. *Journal of Environmental Policy & Planning*, **20**(3), 328–341.

Foucault, M. (1978). *Discipline and Punish: the Birth of the Prison*, New York: Pantheon Books.

Friggens, N. L., Hester, A. J., Mitchell, R. J., Parker, T. C., Subke, J., & Wookey, P. A. (2020). Tree Planting in Organic Soils Does Not Result in Net Carbon Sequestration on Decadal Timescales. *Global Change Biology*, **26**(9), 5178–5188.

Fukuda-Parr, S. (2016). From the Millennium Development Goals to the Sustainable Development Goals: Shifts in Purpose, Concept, and Politics of Global Goal Setting for Development. *Gender & Development*, **24**(1), 43–52.

Fukuda-Parr, S., & McNeill, D. (2019). Knowledge and Politics in Setting and Measuring the SDGs: Introduction to Special Issue. *Global Policy*, **10**(S1), 5–15.

Fukuda-Parr, S., & Muchhala, B. (2020). The Southern Origins of Sustainable Development Goals: Ideas, Actors, Aspirations. *World Development*, **126**, 104706.

Funder, M., & Mweemba, C. E. (2019). Interface Bureaucrats and the Everyday Remaking of Climate Interventions: Evidence from Climate Change Adaptation in Zambia. *Global Environmental Change*, **55**, 130–138. http://dx.doi.org/10.1016/j.gloenvcha.2019.02.007.

Gausset, Q., & Whyte, M. (2012). Climate Change and Land Grab in Africa: Resilience for Whom? In K. Hastrup & K. F. Olwig, eds., *Climate Change and Human Mobility*, 1st edn, Cambridge: Cambridge University Press, pp. 214–234.

Gladwell, M. (2002, July 22). The Talent Myth: Are Smart People Overrated? *The New Yorker*. Retrieved from www.newyorker.com/magazine/2002/07/22/the-talent-myth (accessed June 30, 2025).

Goldman, M. (2005). *Imperial Nature: The World Bank and Struggles for Social Justice in the Age of Globalization*, New Haven, CT: Yale University Press.

Green, M. (2011). Calculating Compassion: Accounting for Some Categorical Practices in International Development. In D. Mosse, ed., *Adventures in Aidland: The Anthropology of Professionals in International Development*, New York: Berghahn Books, pp. 33–56.

Green, W. N., & Baird, I. G. (2020). The Contentious Politics of Hydropower Dam Impact Assessments in the Mekong River Basin. *Political Geography*, **83**, 102272.

Gverdtsiteli, G. (2023). Can Donors Encourage Authoritarian States to Go Green? Evidence from Vietnamese–German Development Cooperation. *The Journal of Environment & Development*, **33**(1), 29–49. http://dx.doi.org/10.1177/10704965231211593.

Hawkins, R. (2012). A New Frontier in Development? The Use of Cause-Related Marketing by International Development Organisations. *Third World Quarterly*, **33**(10), 1783–1801.

Herrmann, S. M., Anyamba, A., & Tucker, C. J. (2005). Recent Trends in Vegetation Dynamics in the African Sahel and Their Relationship to Climate. *Global Environmental Change*, **15**(4), 394–404.

Herrmann, S. M., & Hutchinson, C. F. (2005). The Changing Contexts of the Desertification Debate. *Journal of Arid Environments*, **63**, 538–555.

Ho, K. Z. (2009). *Liquidated: An Ethnography of Wall Street*, Durham, NC: Duke University Press.

Hoben, A. (1995). Paradigms and Politics: The Cultural Construction of Environmental Policy in Ethiopia. *World Development*, **23**(6), 1007–1021.

Horner, R., & Hulme, D. (2019). From International to Global Development: New Geographies of 21st Century Development. *Development and Change*, **50**(2), 347–378.

Howe, J. P. (2014). *Behind the Curve: Science and the Politics of Global Warming*, Seattle: University of Washington Press.

Igoe, J. (2017). *The Nature of Spectacle: On Images, Money, and Conserving Capitalism*, Tuscan: University of Arizona Press.

IPCC (2022). *Climate Change 2022: Impacts, Adaptation and Vulnerability*. Contribution of Working Group II to the Sixth Assessment Report of the Intergovernmental Panel on Climate Change (H.-O. Pörtner, D. C. Roberts, M. Tignor, ... Okem, B. Rama, eds.). Cambridge: Cambridge University Press. http://dx.doi.org/10.1017/9781009325844.

Jamali, D., & Keshishian, T. (2009). Uneasy Alliances: Lessons Learned from Partnerships between Businesses and NGOs in the Context of CSR. *Journal of Business Ethics*, **84**(2), 277–295.

Kapoor, I. (2008). *The Postcolonial Politics of Development*, Abingdon: Routledge.

Kapoor, I. (2013). *Celebrity Humanitarianism: Ideology of Global Charity*, Abingdon: Routledge.

Karnani, A. (2011). "Doing Well by Doing Good": The Grand Illusion. *California Management Review*, **53**(2), 69–86.

Kothari, A., Salleh, A., Escobar, A., Demaria, F., & Acosta, A., eds. (2019). *Pluriverse: A Post-development Dictionary*, New Delhi: Tulika Books and Authorsupfront.

Kothari, U. (2014). Political Discourses of Climate Change and Migration: Resettlement Policies in the Maldives: Political Discourses of Climate Change and Migration. *The Geographical Journal*, **180**(2), 130–140.

Kothari, U., ed. (2019). *A radical History of Development Studies: Individuals, Institutions and Ideologies*, 2nd edn, London: Zed Books.

Kragelund, P. (2019). *South-South Development*, Abingdon: Routledge.

Krauss, W. (2009). Localizing Climate Change: A Multi-sited Approach. In M.-A. Falzon, ed., *Multi-sited Ethnography: Theory, Praxis and Locality in Contemporary Research*, Farnham: Ashgate, pp. 149–164.

Leach, M., & Mearns, R., eds. (1996). *The Lie of the Land: Challenging Received Wisdom on the African Environment*, Oxford: James Currey.

Lejano, R. P., & Nero, S. J. (2020). *The Power of Narrative: Climate Skepticism and the Deconstruction of Science*, 1st edn, Oxford: Oxford University Press. http://dx.doi.org/10.1093/oso/9780197542101.001.0001.

Lekakis, E. J. (2012). Will the Fair Trade Revolution Be Marketised? Commodification, Decommodification and the Political Intensity of Consumer Politics. *Culture and Organization*, **18**(5), 345–358.

Li, T. M. (2007). *The Will to Improve: Governmentality, Development, and the Practice of Politics*, Durham, NC: Duke University Press.

Lindegaard, L. S. (2020) Global Climate Change Knowledge and the Production of Climate Subjects in Vietnam. *Forum for Development Studies*, **47**(1), 157–180, http://dx.doi.org/10.1080/08039410.2019.1685590.

Locher, M., & Sulle, E. (2013). Foreign Land Deals in Tanzania: An Update and a Critical View on the Challenges of Data (Re)production. LDPI Working Paper no. 31. http://dx.doi.org/10.5167/UZH-79407.

Lund, C. (2010). Approaching Development: An Opionated Review. *Progress in Development Studies*, **10**(1), 19–34.

MacDonald, K. I. (2010). Business, Biodiversity and New "Fields" of Conservation: The World Conservation Congress and the Renegotiation of Organisational Order. *Conservation and Society*, **8**(4), 256–275.

Machaqueiro, R. R. (2022). Persistent Connections and Exclusions in Mozambique: From Colonial Anxieties to Contemporary Discourses about the Environment. In P. Stacey, ed., *Global Power and Local Struggles in Developing Countries*, Leiden: Brill, pp. 201–227.

Marcus, G. E. (1995). Ethnography in/of the World System: The Emergence of Multi-sited Ethnography. *Annual Review of Anthropology*, **24**, 95–117.

Marcussen, H. S. (1999). Environmental Paradigms, Knowledge Systems and Policy: The Case of Burkina Faso. *Danish Journal of Geography*, **2**, 93–103.

Maren, M. (1997). *The Road to Hell: The Ravaging Effects of Foreign Aid and International Charity*, New York: Free Press.

Marino, E., & Ribot, J. (2012). Special Issue Introduction: Adding Insult to Injury: Climate Change and the Inequities of Climate Intervention. *Global Environmental Change*, **22**(2), 323–328. http://dx.doi.org/10.1016/j.gloenvcha.2012.03.001.

Martin, D. A., Llopis, J. C., Raveloaritiana, E., ... Zaehringer, J. G. (2023). Drivers and Consequences of Archetypical Shifting Cultivation Transitions. *People and Nature*, 5(2), 529–541.

Mawdsley, E. (2017). Development Geography 1: Cooperation, Competition and Convergence between "North" and "South." *Progress in Human Geography*, **41**(1), 108–117.

Mawdsley, E. (2018). "From Billions to Trillions": Financing the SDGs in a World "Beyond Aid." *Dialogues in Human Geography*, **8**(2), 191–195.

McKenna, C. D. (2006). *The World's Newest Profession: Management Consulting in the Twentieth Century*, Cambridge: Cambridge University Press. https://doi.org/10.1017/CBO9780511511622.

Menga, F., & Goodman, M. K. (2022). The High Priests of Global Development: Capitalism, Religion and the Political Economy of Sacrifice in a Celebrity-Led Water Charity. *Development and Change*, **53**(4), 705–735.

Merchant, C. (2013). *Reinventing Eden: The Fate of Nature in Western Culture*, 2nd edn, Abingdon: Routledge.

Merriam-Webster. (2023). "Salvation." *Merriam-Webster Dictionary*. Retrieved from www.merriam-webster.com/dictionary/salvation (accessed January 25, 2023).

Merry, S. E. (2019). The Sustainable Development Goals Confront the Infrastructure of Measurement. *Global Policy*, **10**(S1), 146–148.

Mikulewicz, M. (2020). The Discursive Politics of Adaptation to Climate Change. *Annals of the American Association of Geographers*, **110**(6), 1807–1830. http://dx.doi.org/10.1080/24694452.2020.1736981.

Miller, F. (2018). Material, Discursive and Cultural Framings of Water in Southeast Asian Development. In A. McGregor, L. Law, & F. Miller, eds., *Routledge Handbook of Southeast Asian Development*, Abingdon: Routledge, pp. 285–299.

Mills-Novoa, M., Boelens, R., Hoogesteger, J., & Vos, J. (2020) Governmentalities, Hydrosocial Territories & Recognition Politics: The Making of Objects and Subjects for Climate Change Adaptation in Ecuador. *Geoforum*, **115**, 90–101. http://dx.doi.org/10.1016/j.geoforum.2020.06.024.

Mills-Novoa, M., Boelens, R., Hoogesteger, J., & Vos, J. (2023). Resisting, Leveraging, and Reworking Climate Change Adaptation Projects from Below: Placing Adaptation in Ecuador's Agrarian Struggle. *The Journal of Peasant Studies*, **50**(6), 2283–2311. http://dx.doi.org/10.1080/03066150.2022.2144252.

Moseley, W. G., & Laris, P. (2008). West African Environmental Narratives and Development-Volunteer Praxis. *Geographical Review*, **98**(1), 59–81.

Moser, S. C., & Hart, J. A. F. (2015). The Long Arm of Climate Change: Societal Teleconnections and the Future of Climate Change Impacts Studies. *Climatic Change*, **129**, 13–26. http://dx.doi.org/10.1007/s10584-015-1328-z.

Mosse, D. (2006). Anti-social Anthropology? Objectivity, Objection, and the Ethnography of Public Policy and Professional Communities. *Journal of the Royal Anthropological Institute*, **12**(4), 935–956.

Mosse, D. (2011). Introduction: The Anthropology of Expertise and Professionals in International Development. In *Adventures in Aidland: The Anthropology of Professionals in International Development*, New York: Berghahn Books, pp. 1–31.

Mosse, D., & Lewis, D. (2006). Theoretical Approaches to Brokerage and Translation in Development. In D. Lewis & D. Mosse, eds., *Development Brokers and Translators: The Ethnography of Aid and Agencies*, Bloomfield, CT: Kumarian Press, pp. 1–26.

Mostafanezhad, M. (2013). ""Getting in Touch with Your Inner Angelina": Celebrity Humanitarianism and the Cultural Politics of Gendered Generosity in Volunteer Tourism. *Third World Quarterly*, **34**(3), 485–499.

Mostafanezhad, M. (2014). Volunteer Tourism and the Popular Humanitarian Gaze. *Geoforum*, **54**, 111–118.

Mosurska, A., Clark-Ginsberg, A., Sallu, S., & Ford, J. (2023). Disasters and Indigenous Peoples: A Critical Discourse Analysis of the Expert News Media. *Environment and Planning E: Nature and Space*, **6**(1), 178–201.

Mutua, M. (2001). Savages, Victims, and Saviors: The Metaphor of Human Rights. *Harward International Law Journal*, **1**(42), 201–245.

Mwamfupe, A., Olwig, M. F., Silvano, P., Brockington, D., & Henriksen, L. F. (2022). 5 Sustainability Partnerships in the Forestry Sector in South-east Tanzania. In S. Ponte, C. Noe, & D. Brockington, eds., *Contested Sustainability: The Political Ecology of Conservation and Development in*

Tanzania, Oxford: James Currey, pp. 143–161. https://doi.org/10.2307/j.ctv2x4kp1m.11.

Nader, L. (1972). Up the Anthropologist: Perspectives Gained from Studying Up. In D. Hymes, ed., *Reinventing Anthropology*, New York: Pantheon Books, pp. 284–311.

Nielsen, J. Ø. (2010). The Outburst: Climate Change, Gender Relations, and Situational Analysis. *Social Analysis*, **54**(3), 76–89. http://dx.doi.org/10.3167/sa.2010.540305.

Nielsen, J. Ø., D'haen, S., & Reenberg, A. (2012). Adaptation to Climate Change as a Development Project: A Case Study from Northern Burkina Faso. *Climate and Development*, **4**(1), 16–25.

Nightingale, A. J., Eriksen, S., Taylor, M., … Whitfield, S. (2020). Beyond Technical Fixes: Climate Solutions and the Great Derangement. *Climate and Development*, **12**(4), 343–352. http://dx.doi.org/10.1080/17565529.2019.1624495.

Noe, C. (2013). *Contesting Village Land: Uranium and Sport Hunting in Mbarang'andu Wildlife Management Area, Tanzania*. LDPI Working Paper no. 15.

Olivier de Sardan, J.-P. (2005). *Anthropology and Development: Understanding Contemporary Social Change*, London: Zed Books.

Olivier de Sardan, J.-P. (2021). *La revanche des contextes: des mésaventures de l'ingénierie sociale, en Afrique et au-delà*, Paris: Éditions Karthala.

Olwig, K. F. (2007). *Caribbean Journeys: An Ethnography of Migration and Home in Three Family Networks*, Durham, NC: Duke University Press.

Olwig, K. R. (2021 [1984]). *Nature's Ideological Landscape: A Literary and Geographic Perspective on its Development and Preservation on Denmark's Jutland Heath*, Abingdon: Routledge.

Olwig, M. F. (2009). Climate Change = Discourse Change? Development and Relief Organizations' Use of the Concept of Resilience. In K. Hastrup, ed., *The Question of Resilience: Social Responses to Climate Change*, København: Det Kongelige Danske Videnskabernes Selskab, pp. 314–335. Retrieved from http://publ.royalacademy.dk/backend/web/uploads/2020-02-14/AFL%206/H_106_00_00_2009_2633/H_106_15_00_2009_2648.pdf (accessed July 23, 2025).

Olwig, M. F. (2012). Multi-sited Resilience: The Mutual Construction of "Local" and "Global" Understandings and Practices of Adaptation and Innovation. *Applied Geography*, **33**, 112–118. https://doi.org/10.1016/j.apgeog.2011.10.007.

Olwig, M. F. (2013). Beyond Translation: Reconceptualizing the Role of Local Practitioners and the Development "Interface." *The European Journal of Development Research*, **25**(3), 428–444. https://doi.org/10.1057/ejdr.2013.9.

Olwig, M. F. (2021a). Introduction: Commodifying Humanitarian Sentiments? The Black Box of the For-profit and Non-profit Partnership. *World Development*, **145**, 105536. https://doi.org/10.1016/j.worlddev.2021.105536.

Olwig, M. F. (2021b). Sustainability Superheroes? For-profit Narratives of "Doing Good" in the Era of the SDGs. *World Development*, **142**, 105427. https://doi.org/10.1016/j.worlddev.2021.105427.

Olwig, M. F., Asare, R., Meilby, H., Vaast, P., & Owusu, K. (2024a). Introduction: Climate, Cocoa and Trees. In M. F. Olwig, A. S. Bosselman, & K. Owusu, eds., *Agroforestry as Climate Change Adaptation: The Case of Cocoa Farming in Ghana*, London: Palgrave Macmillan, pp. 1–33. https://doi.org/10.1007/978-3-031-45635-0_1.

Olwig, M. F., Asare, R., Vaast, P., & Bosselman, A. S. (2024b). Can Agroforestry Provide a Future for Cocoa? Implications for Policy and Practice. In M. F. Olwig, A. S. Bosselman, & K. Owusu, eds., *Agroforestry as Climate Change Adaptation: The Case of Cocoa Farming in Ghana*, London: Palgrave Macmillan, pp. 147–166. https://doi.org/10.1007/978-3-031-45635-0_6.

Olwig, M. F., Bosselman, A. S., & Owusu, K., eds. (2024c). *Agroforestry as Climate Change Adaptation: The Case of Cocoa Farming in Ghana*, London: Palgrave Macmillan. https://doi.org/10.1007/978-3-031-45635-0.

Olwig, M. F., & Christiansen, L. B. (2015). Irony and Politically Incorrect Humanitarianism: Danish Celebrity-led Benefit Events. In L. A. Richey, *Celebrity Humanitarianism and North-South Relations: Politics, Place and Power*, Abingdon: Routledge, pp. 170–188. https://doi.org/10.4324/9781315721187-11.

Olwig, M. F., & Christiansen, L. B. (2016). Festive Environmentalism: A Carnevalesque Reading of Eco-voluntourism at the Roskilde Festival. In M. Mostafanezhad, R. Norum, E. J. Shelton, & A. Thompson-Carr, *Political Ecology of Tourism: Community, Power and the Environment*, Abingdon: Routledge, pp. 108–128.

Olwig, M. F., & Gough, K. V. (2013). Basket Weaving and Social Weaving: Young Ghanaian Artisans' Mobilization of Resources through Mobility in Times of Climate Change. *Geoforum*, **45**, 168–177. https://doi.org/10.1016/j.geoforum.2012.11.001.

Olwig, M. F., Noe, C., Kangalawe, R., & Luoga, E. (2015). Inverting the Moral Economy: The Case of Land Acquisitions for Forest Plantations in Tanzania.

Third World Quarterly, **36**(12), 2316–2336. https://doi.org/10.1080/01436597.2015.1078231.

Olwig, M. F., & Rasmussen, L. V. (2016). West African Waterworlds: Narratives of Absence versus Narratives of Excess. In K. Hastrup & F. Hastrup, eds., *Waterworlds: Anthropology in Fluid Environments*, New York Oxford: Berghahn, pp. 110–128.

Olwig, M. F., Sørensen, M. K., Rasmussen, M. S., ... Karunagaran, V. M. (2007). Using Remote Sensing to Assess the Protective Role of Coastal Woody Vegetation against Tsunami Waves. *International Journal of Remote Sensing*, **28**(13–14), 3153–3169. https://doi.org/10.1080/01431160701420597.

Osaka S., Bellamy, R. & Castree, N. (2021) Framing "Nature-Based" Solutions to Climate Change. *WIREs Climate Change* 12(5), e729. https://doi.org/10.1002/wcc.729.

Paprocki, K. (2018). Threatening Dystopias: Development and Adaptation Regimes in Bangladesh. *Annals of the American Association of Geographers*, **108**(4), 955–973. http://dx.doi.org/10.1080/24694452.2017.1406330.

Paulson, S. (2019). Pluriversal Learning: Pathways toward a World of many worlds. *Nordia Geographical Publications*, **47**(5), 85–109.

Pigg, S. L. (1992). Inventing Social Categories through Place: Social Representations and Development in Nepal. *Comparative Studies in Society and History*, **34**(3), 491–513.

Ponte, S. (2019). *Business, Power and Sustainability in a World of Global Value Chains*, London: Zed Books.

Postill, J. (2024). Doing Digital Ethnography: A Comparison of Two Social Movement Studies. In L. Cox, A. Szolucha, A. A. Lozano, & S. Chattopadhyay, eds., *Handbook of Research Methods and Applications for Social Movements*, Cheltenham: Edward Elgar Publishing, pp. 144–158.

Pruce, J. R. (2016). What Does Human Rights Look Like? The Visual Culture of Aid, Advocacy, and Activism. In M. Monshipouri, ed., *Information Politics, Protests, and Human Rights in the Digital Age*, Cambridge: Cambridge University Press, pp. 50–72.

Prudham, S. (2009). Pimping Climate Change: Richard Branson, Global Warming, and the Performance of Green Capitalism. *Environment and Planning A: Economy and Space*, **41**(7), 1594–1613.

Purdon, M. (2013). Land Acquisitions in Tanzania: Strong Sustainability, Weak Sustainability and the Importance of Comparative Methods. *Journal of Agricultural and Environmental Ethics*, **26**(6), 1127–1156.

Rasmussen, L. V., Watkins, C., & Agrawal, A. (2017). Forest Contributions to Livelihoods in Changing Agriculture-Forest Landscapes. *Forest Policy and Economics*, **84**, 1–8.

Richey, L. A. (2014). Toward New Knowledges in Development: New Actors and Alliances. *Forum for Development Studies*, **41**(3), 551–563.

Richey, L. A., & Brockington, D. (2020). Celebrity Humanitarianism: Using Tropes of Engagement to Understand North/South Relations. *Perspectives on Politics*, 18(1), 43–59.

Richey, L. A., & Ponte, S. (2011). *Brand Aid: Shopping Well to Save the World*, Minneapolis: University of Minnesota Press.

Roe, E. M. (1991). Development Narratives, or Making the Best of Blueprint Development. *World Development*, **19**(4), 287–300.

Rossi, B. (2006). Aid Policies and Recipient Strategies in Niger: Why Donors and Recipients Should Not Be Compartmentalized into Separate "Worlds of Knowledge." In D. Lewis & D. Mosse, eds., *Development Brokers and Translators: The Ethnography of Aid and Agencies*, Bloomfield, CT: Kumarian Press, pp. 27–49.

Sachs, J., Schmidt-Traub, G., Kroll, C., Lafortune, G., & Fuller, G. (2019). *Sustainable Development Report 2019*, New York: Bertelsmann Stiftung and Sustainable Development Solutions Network (SDSN).

Said, E. W. (1978). *Orientalism*, 1st edn, New York: Pantheon Books.

Salazar, N. B. (2011). The Power of Imagination in Transnational Mobilities. *Identities*, **18**(6), 576–598.

Scheyvens, R., Banks, G., & Hughes, E. (2016). The Private Sector and the SDGs: The Need to Move Beyond "Business as Usual." *Sustainable Development*, **24**(6), 371–382.

Scott, J. C. (1998). *Seeing Like a State: How Certain Schemes to Improve the Human Condition Have Failed*, New Haven, CT: Yale University Press.

Sen, S. (2020a). *Decolonizing Palestine: Hamas between the Anticolonial and the Postcolonial*, Ithaca, NY: Cornell University Press.

Sen, S. (2020b). On Colonial Self-perceptions: The European Union, Turkey and the "Bad" Leader. *Interventions*, **22**(6), 763–782. https://doi.org/10.1080/1369801X.2020.1749706.

Shivji, I. G. (2009). *Accumulation in an African Periphery: A Theoretical Framework*, Dar es Salaam: Mkuki na Nyota Publishers.

Silveira, L., & Alonso, J. (2009). Runoff Modifications Due to the Conversion of Natural Grasslands to Forests in a Large Basin in Uruguay. *Hydrological Processes*, **23**(2), 320–329.

Songsore, J. (2011). *Regional Development in Ghana: The Theory and the Reality*, new edn, Accra: Woeli Publishing Services.

Sørensen, B. R. (2008). Humanitarian NGOs and Mediations of Political Order in Sri Lanka. *Critical Asian Studies*, **40**(1), 113–142.

Sultana, F. (2022). The Unbearable Heaviness of Climate Coloniality. *Political Geography*, **99**, 102638.

Svarstad, H., & Benjaminsen, T. A. (2017). Nothing Succeeds Like Success Narratives: A Case of Conservation and Development in the Time of REDD. *Journal of Eastern African Studies*, **11**(3), 482–505.

Townsend J., Moola, F., & Craig, M.-K. (2020) Indigenous Peoples Are Critical to the Success of Nature-Based Solutions to Climate Change. *FACETS* **5**(1), 551–556. https://doi.org/10.1139/facets-2019-0058.

Tran, P., Marincioni, F., & Shaw, R. (2010). Catastrophic Flood and Forest Cover Change in the Huong River Basin, Central Viet Nam: A Gap between Common Perceptions and Facts. *Journal of Environmental Management*, **91**(11), 2186–2200.

Tran, P., Marincioni, F., Shaw, R., Sarti, M., & van An, L. (2008). Flood Risk Management in Central Viet Nam: Challenges and Potentials. *Natural Hazards*, **46**(1), 119–138.

Tran, T. A., & Rodela, R. (2019). Integrating Farmers' Adaptive Knowledge into Flood Management and Adaptation Policies in the Vietnamese Mekong Delta: A Social Learning Perspective. *Global Environmental Change*, **55**, 84–96.

Tschakert, P., Sagoe, R., Ofori-Darko, G., & Codjoe, S. N. (2010). Floods in the Sahel: An Analysis of Anomalies, Memory, and Anticipatory Learning. *Climatic Change*, **103**(3–4), 471–502.

United Nations. (n.d.). Revitalize the Global Partnership for Sustainable Development. Sustainable Development Goals. Retrieved from www.un.org/sustainabledevelopment/globalpartnerships/ (accessed July 11, 2025).

UN-REDD Programme. (2016). UN-REDD Programme Fact Sheet: About REDD+. Retrieved from www.un-redd.org/sites/default/files/2021-10/Fact%20Sheet%201-%20About%20REDD3.pdf (accessed July 1, 2025).

van Zanten, J. A., & van Tulder, R. (2018). Multinational Enterprises and the Sustainable Development Goals: An Institutional Approach to Corporate Engagement. *Journal of International Business Policy*, **1**(3–4), 208–233.

Vestergaard, A. (2008). Humanitarian Branding and the Media: The case of Amnesty International. *Journal of Language and Politics*, **3**, 471–493.

Whitehead, A. (2006). Persistent Poverty in North East Ghana. *Journal of Development Studies*, **42**(2), 278–300.

Wilhelmova, V. (2022, November 20). COP27 Closes with Deal on Loss and Damage: "A Step towards Justice," Says UN Chief. Retrieved from https://news.un.org/en/story/2022/11/1130832 (accessed July 1, 2025).

Wisner, B., Blaikie, P., Cannon, T., & Davis, I. (2004). *At Risk: Natural Hazards, People's Vulnerability and Disasters*, 2nd edn., Abingdon: Routledge.

Ziegler, A. D., Phelps, J., Yuen, J. Q., . . . Koh, L. P. (2012). Carbon Outcomes of Major Land-Cover Transitions in SE Asia: Great Uncertainties and REDD + Policy Implications. *Global Change Biology*, **18**(10), 3087–3099.

Zink, E. (2013). *Hot Science, High Water: Assembling Nature, Society and Environmental Policy in Contemporary Vietnam*, Copenhagen: NIAS Press.

Acknowledgements

First, I am very thankful for the willingness of the farmers, practitioners, donors, scientists, businesspeople, government employees, local administrators and village leaders to participate in my research, for being helpful and welcoming, and for their invaluable insights. I would also like to thank all the colleagues who have given me valuable feedback, including all the principal investigators and co-investigators in the different research projects I have been part of in the years I have been doing the research drawn upon in this Element, and my colleagues at Roskilde University, particularly the International Development Research Group and Camilla Riel. Additionally, Lisa Ann Richey, Stefano Ponte, Kirsten Hastrup, Katherine Gough, Birgitte Refslund Sørensen, Cecilie Rubow, Laura Vang Rasmussen, Frida Hastrup, Christine Noe, Melissa Leach, Anthony Bebbington, Jytte Agergaard, Uma Kothari, Ole Bruun, Dan Brockington, Peter Kragelund, Lindsay Whitfield, Lene Bull Christiansen, Lars Buur, Bjørn Thomassen, Laura Portwood, Thilde Langevang, Anne Vestergaard, Christian Lund, Alexandra Budabin, Maha Rafi Atal, Janette Kotivirta, Sofie Elbæk Henriksen, Roberta Hawkins, Michael Goodman and Jean-Pierre Olivier de Sardan have provided very helpful comments, inspiration and/or mentorship. I also thank my editor Arun Agrawal for his significant inputs, support and guidance and for the anonymous reviewers' constructive comments. Moreover, I am grateful for the support received from The Carlsberg Foundation through a monograph fellowship grant (CF21-0402) that enabled me to write this Element and a publication grant (CF25-0451) that helped make the Element open access.

I would also like to acknowledge and thank the funding bodies that have made my research through the years possible. These are the European Research Council ("Waterworlds: Natural Environmental Disasters and Social Resilience in Anthropological Perspective," grant 229459), The Independent Research Fund Denmark ("Commodifying Compassion: Implications of Turning People and Humanitarian Causes Into Marketable Things," grant 6109-00158B; "Universal Aspirations vs. Geopolitical Divides: Imagining the World as a 'Post-Millennial' in the SDG Era," grant 1053-00029B) and the Danida Fellowship Center ("Climate Smart Cocoa Systems for Ghana, CLIMCOCOA," grant 16-P02-GHA; "Climate Change-Induced Water Disaster and Participatory Information System for Vulnerability Reduction in North Central Vietnam," grant 11-P04-VIE; "Entailments of Large-Scale Land Investments on Agriculture and Food Security in Mufindi East, Tanzania," grant BSU-GEP 32663; "NEPSUS: New Partnerships For Sustainability," grant 16–01-CBS). Last, but not least, thank you to my family, my parents Karen and Kenneth, my husband Som, and my children Shaan and Sonia, for being my village and for being good storytellers.

About the Author

Mette Fog Olwig, Associate Professor at Roskilde University, Denmark, does research on perceptions, narratives and experiences of climate change, natural disasters and development. She pays particular attention to their consequences for sustainability policies and practices. She has conducted multi-sited ethnographic fieldwork and scientific research among different actors, including development practitioners, donors, local administrators, businesspeople, farmers and youth in Ghana, Vietnam, Tanzania, the US and Denmark. She is the co-editor of *Agroforestry as Climate Change Adaptation* (Palgrave 2024). Her articles have been published in journals such as *Science, World Development, Global Environmental Change, Geoforum* and *Applied Geography*.

Cambridge Elements

Sustainability: Science, Policy, Practice

Series Editor-in-Chief
Arun Agrawal
University of Notre Dame

Arun Agrawal is the Pulte Family Professor of Development Policy at the Keough School of Global Affairs and the inaugural director of the Just Transformations to Sustainability Initiative at the University of Notre Dame. His research focuses on the political economy of human-environment interactions and systems, sustainability of social-ecological systems, governance of natural resources, inter-temporal and cross-scale dynamics of socio-environmental changes, and the relationship of climate and environmental stressors with conflict, inequality, and health.

Advisory Editorial Board
Neil Adger, *University of Exeter*
Anthony Bebbington, *The Ford Foundation*
Christoph Bene, *Alliance Bioversity International*
William Clark, *Harvard University*
Ruth S. DeFries, *Columbia University*
Melissa Leach, *University of Sussex*
Diana Liverman, *University of Arizona*
Yadvinder Malhi, *University of Oxford*
Debra Rowe, *Oakland Community College*
B. L. Turner II, *Arizona State University*
Esther Turnhout, *University of Twente*

Editorial Board
Vanesa Castan Broto, *The University of Sheffield*
Paul J. Ferraro, *Johns Hopkins University*
Reetika Khera, *Indian Institute of Technology Delhi*
Myanna Lahsen, *Linkoping University*
Christian Lund, *University of Copenhagen*
Johan Oldekop, *University of Manchester*
Laura Vang Rasmussen, *University of Copenhagen*
Diana Ürge-Vorsatz, *Central European University*

About the Series
This series showcases scholarship that investigates persistent, multi-scale challenges to global sustainability. It facilitates the consolidation of the science and social science of sustainability, bridging the gap between knowledge, policy, and practice. It aims to include the best reviews of relevant themes related to environment, development, and sustainability.

Cambridge Elements

Sustainability: Science, Policy, Practice

Elements in the Series

Girl Power: Sustainability, Empowerment, and Justice
Jin In

Climate Change on Trial
César Rodríguez-Garavito

How To Normatively Transform Food Systems
Abdul-Rahim Abdulai and Christophe Béné

A Bit Too Simple: Narratives of Development, Sustainability and Climate Change
Mette Fog Olwig

A full series listing is available at: www.cambridge.org/ESBL

For EU product safety concerns, contact us at Calle de José Abascal, 56–1°,
28003 Madrid, Spain or eugpsr@cambridge.org.

www.ingramcontent.com/pod-product-compliance
Lightning Source LLC
LaVergne TN
LVHW021944060526
838200LV00042B/1915